Forgive Who?

The Struggle to Obey

God's Awful Command

*To Julia:
My sister, my friend.
Love,
Rev. Ann*

A Sacred Closet Book

Forgive Who?
The Struggle to Obey God's Awful Command

By Dr. Susan K. Williams Smith
Edited by Donna Marie Williams

A Sacred Closet Book

FORGIVE WHO?
The Publishing Institute, Inc.
Chicago, Illinois

Cover and layout by Harrison Williams

Scripture quotations are from New International Version (NIV) unless otherwise noted.

Manufactured in the United States of America

Library of Congress Control Number: 2003107728
ISBN: 1-4125-4998-1

For information: THE PUBLISHING INSTITUTE, INC.
                     P. O. Box 43048
                     Chicago, Illinois 60643

Dedication

This book is dedicated to everyone who has ever wrestled with the divine requirement of forgiveness and to those who have chosen to ignore the command as well. As with every book I write, this book is also dedicated to my children, Caroline and Charlie, who forever and constantly remind me to practice what I preach and teach, especially about forgiveness.

Acknowledgements

I would first like to acknowledge God for always feeding and sustaining me in rough times and allowing me the gift of joy in other times. He alone allows me life, which in turn allows me the opportunity to acknowledge people without whom I could not move on:

Ida Edmondson, who urged me to move forward on this work and who always urges me to move forward, no matter what. I can hear you sighing a sigh of relief even as I write this because I managed to push past myself. You always encourage me to do that, no matter what's going on in your life.

Diane Williams, a friend, sister, and true seeker of God. Rarely have I seen such growth in a person as you've demonstrated. You'll never know how much I look forward to our daily conversations.

Gwen Edwards and Brenda Evans, who offer me more love and support than I deserve. My life is better for knowing you both. The church is better for having you there.

Denise Stinson and Rev. Dr. Renita Weems, whose encouragement made me move forward. Do you guys know how inspiring it was to hear from you, that I had a little potential as a writer? I thank you both.

Janice Williams and Donna Marie Williams, my publisher and editor. I still don't know how we hooked up, Janice. I just know that God was in it and is in it. Janice, I thank you for believing this book was worth being published. Donna, you have been more than priceless in the editing of this book. You have both encouraged and inspired me.

And finally, my parents, now gone and who always believed I should write. It's taken a while, but this book is a gift to you both.

Table of Contents

Foreword

Forgiveness is a difficult process. It is at the center of the message of the Christian faith, yet it is one of the most difficult tasks a Christian is challenged to carry out on a daily and ongoing basis. Dr. Susan Smith has tackled this difficult task and ongoing challenge in an exciting and engaging manner in this book.

She writes from the perspective of a Pastor, a professor and a single parent. She writes out of the pain she has experienced and she writes from the perspective of one who knows personally how difficult the demands of Jesus are.

The power in her writing, however, combined with the humor, the love and the passion she has for God and God's people make reading this book an unforgettable experience. *Forgive Who?* is a roadmap for transformation and a "must read" for those who are serious about following Him who asks us to forgive others as we have been forgiven by God.

Rev. Jeremiah A. Wright, Jr., Senior Pastor
Trinity United Church of Christ, Chicago, Illinois

Introduction

"AND WHEN YOU STAND PRAYING, IF YOU HOLD ANYTHING AGAINST ANYONE, FORGIVE HIM, SO THAT YOUR FATHER IN HEAVEN MAY FORGIVE YOU YOUR SINS."

—MARK 11:25

It's the most impossible of all the commands Jesus gives: to forgive those who have done us wrong.

What could He have been thinking? After all, we're human beings, with all of the attendant flaws. He knows how we are. Surely the Father whispered to Him that it was because of our flaws that He, Jesus, had to come here.

We have many shortcomings, but our biggest are the inability and unwillingness to forgive people who have hurt us. If the truth be told, not only are we unwilling to forgive others, but we are frequently unwilling and unable to forgive ourselves. It's just how we're wired.

So what's up with the command? Only Jesus was so good and forgiving that He could say **while hanging on the cross**, "Father, forgive them, for they know not what they do." But as God's Son, wasn't He supposed to be able to do that?

You say we're God's children, too? Well, yes, but far removed, don't you think? There's something about being the product of the Immaculate Conception that gave Jesus more chutzpah, yes? I mean, not even God's very first created humans, Adam and Eve, had Jesus' strength, not to mention his divinity. And how about their children? Was forgiveness in Cain's heart? Hardly. Nor was forgiveness in the hearts of the folks who succeeded him.

So, what's the deal? Jesus knew when He said it that this command to forgive was not going to fly. He knew that we'd politely read those scriptures and move to other, less troubling passages. He knew that we'd rationalize our inability and unwillingness to forgive by saying that God looks beyond our faults and sees our needs. He knew that we'd trust in His grace to save us *just in case* we didn't have the power or strength to forgive. So, why did He put that command in the prayer most Christians say every Sunday, the Lord's Prayer: "… and forgive us our trespasses as we forgive those who trespass against us." Yeah, right. That's the biggest lie we say every week, next to "Thy will be done."

What was God's motive for giving us this command that's so distasteful to us? Surely there had to be a reason that we don't yet understand. Perhaps it was because Jesus could see that the people around Him, though they loved Him, had real issues with forgiveness. They were more concerned with "justice," or making sure someone "gets it" for doing bad things. Then, as now, people thought that forgiveness was an option and not a necessity. So Jesus, knowing the importance of forgiveness in the very health and life of people, decided to highlight this command in all of His teachings.

Why do we have to forgive? It's too hard. It's too stupid. If we forgive the people who walk all over us, they'll smirk and say we're pathetic. Worse, they'll walk all over us again and again because they know we're trying to get to heaven or some such. They'll laugh at us, Jesus! Surely you know.

Forgiving is too hard on the ego. Can you imagine even speaking to the person who hurt you so badly, let alone *forgiving* him or her? "Forgive who? Frankly, there isn't anything to say. The damage has been done. It was done a long time ago, and it's too late to try to fix it now." Such might be the thoughts of Christians who are struggling to follow the commands of the Christ.

Forgiving people is distasteful to us, and honestly, we ignore the command. We even try to reinterpret or redefine what Jesus meant, glossing over what He forthrightly said about forgiveness. We steer ourselves and others to more comfortable scriptures, like the ones found in the Old Testament about it being okay to seek "an eye for an eye." Or we can always fall back on the "we're only human" rationalization.

The Bible doesn't support our rationalizations. Neither does the Torah nor the Koran. A long time ago Alexander Pope wrote, "To err is human, to forgive, divine." Surely he did not jest. The human stuff is easy. It's the command to forgive that's tough—but necessary for our peace while on earth and for establishing a real connection with God.

Actually, it makes us angry to think that God would want us to forgive the man who raped and killed our daughter. Or the teens that went on a wild rampage, shooting and killing innocent teachers and students in a school building. It's absolutely infuriating to think that God would *require* us to forgive a father or an uncle who molested us, or a mother who was told about the indiscretions but didn't do a thing because she didn't want to lose her financial security.

To think that God or His son, Jesus, would want us to forgive the masterminds behind the September 11, 2001 attacks on the World Trade Center and the Pentagon is difficult to swallow. Come on, God! Innocent people died! Wives and children must now live without their husbands and fathers, and we're supposed to say, "Father, forgive them?" I don't think so. I don't want to.

It goes against the grain to forgive the husband who deserted his wife of 21 years to marry a woman half his age or the man who was never there for his children. It wouldn't show strength to forgive the person who actively and boldly worked to make your pastorate fail. Only a wimp would welcome back a liar who tried to destroy his marriage or friendship.

Have the Jews forgiven the Nazis for the Holocaust? Are they supposed to? It's a fact that African Americans have not forgiven whites for the injustices hurled against them since they set foot on American soil. Can forgiveness make the past go away? Can it wipe the slate clean? Can it make the wrongs right? No, you say, to all of those questions. Then what's the use of forgiveness?

Garrett Keizer writes, "There is for the Christian, or for at least this Christian, an additional source of anger and outrage: the mere suggestion that any person who has suffered such a thing ought to forgive the persons who inflicted it."[1] He was referring to a white South African woman who was beaten and raped by a gang of white youths who didn't approve of her serving black patrons in her store. After they violated her, they carved the letter "k" on her breast, as if to forever remind her of her atrocity. The letter "k" represented the first letter of the Afrikaans word "kaffir," which means nigger.

And we're supposed to *forgive* these guys?

Another instance of blatant evil was the case of Abner Louima. Louima, a Haitian immigrant who lived in New York City, happened to be in the wrong place at the wrong time. New York officers Justin Volpe, Charles Schwarz, Thomas Bruder, and Thomas Wiese arrested him outside a Brooklyn nightclub. The officers said they thought Louima was armed and dangerous, but he wasn't. Prosecutors charged that Louima was beaten while in the patrol car and sexually assaulted in the precinct bathroom. One officer held him down while another sodomized him with a wooden stick. When he recovered, he identified the officers who had beaten him. They were tried and convicted. Three of the convictions were overturned; Justin Volpe, however, pleaded guilty to the actual brutality and is still in prison.

The crime against Louima was horrific. Jesus says we're to forgive and forget. Now come on, Jesus. How are Mr. Louima and his family *really* supposed to do that? How, pray tell?

How do you forgive when your very soul has been violated and stripped apart? How does the young woman who was molested as a girl and now cannot have a decent sexual relationship—how does she forgive? When she looks at the offender and remembers what he did to her, when she realizes how her past pain prevents her from fully loving her husband, how does she forgive? Why do You expect it? How do you forgive a mother or father who was so physically, verbally, and emotionally abusive that the grown child has little chance for a healthy life? How do we move past our hurts to even wanting to forgive?

I can hear Jesus sighing. Where's your faith? Where's the faith that reminds you that you really can do all things through Christ, even forgive the seemingly unforgivable? This forgiving thing isn't a human ability. It's a divine gift that's freely given, but we have to ask God for it. We have to hold out our hands to receive it.

Jesus is asking us, "Why won't you trust me enough to take the gift? Don't you know that forgiveness is not for the people who have offended you, but for *you?* Why won't you let me be your Savior, truly and completely? In order to be saved, you have to do what I tell you to do. You can't chart your own course with me as an advisor. Don't you remember what I said? "I am the *Way.*" (John 14:6) Don't you understand that unless you forgive, or at least try to, you're following the wrong Way? Don't you understand that your unwillingness to forgive is blocking our relationship from being all that it can be?"

Alas, we can't hear Jesus sighing, nor do we want to. Our human will fights against the divine spirit, which is trying to make an impression on and heal our wounded spirits.

We live in agony when we don't have to, hating people and resenting people, even ourselves, when it's so unnecessary. We're missing out on the gift of salvation—feeling the power and presence of God while we're alive. We miss out on the "perfect peace," (Isaiah 26:3) which is a big part of the salvation experience. Jesus came here so "that [we] may have life, and have it to the full." (John 10:10) This is also what salvation is all about. Do you really think you have to die to experience salvation? Do you understand that in order to receive salvation, you really do have to meet Jesus' expectations?

Introduction

It seems that we don't get it, and this causes Jesus to weep.

This book will take us to the edge of our own chasms of grudge holding, anger, and despair—the chasms we put between ourselves and God, Jesus, peace, joy, and deliverance. We'll go to the edge of those chasms and face ourselves and our issues of forgiveness.

The practice of forgiveness can feel like a wilderness journey. Why? Because we don't know what to expect. We don't know where God will take us and how we'll be affected. We know how we feel right now, and though it might not be comfortable, it's at least familiar. If we agree to enter into the process of forgiveness, we'll face the fears that always accompany the unknown.

Not long ago I was training for a marathon in Atlanta. I didn't know the area, and dusk was fast approaching. As I ran, I didn't see a traffic light or a four-way stop sign for what seemed like miles. When I finally did, I was hit with a wave of anxiety. What if the crossroad at the light didn't lead me back home? What if I took a wrong turn and ended up lost? It was getting dark, and I didn't have any identification on me, nor did I have my cell phone. I was too afraid to move on; I turned around and retraced my steps. Later, I found out that if I had made a right turn at that light, I would have soon come to a street I recognized.

That's the nature of this walk. We're entering into an unknown territory, and nothing about it will be familiar. We won't be able to see around the corner or predict where we'll end up. How will we be received, not by God, but by our peers? Are people going to talk about us? Will we be accused of being wimps? Will offenders become smug as we offer forgiveness to them? Will they try to hurt us again and again because they think we're easy prey? Will we really feel better if we forgive? Are there any guarantees?

As you struggle with the desire to stop and go back to what's familiar, ask yourself, "Do I want to be healed?" Agreeing to move forward, in spite of the unfamiliar nature of the path, will lift you upward, closer to God. I hope that you won't let fear and anxiety get the best of you and make you stop the journey or turn back. The mere idea of having to forgive someone you don't even want to think about might turn you off to the practice of forgiveness, but I hope you'll reconsider.

Forgive Who?

For those of you who are ready to forgive, I hope you'll fuel your spirits with prayers because you'll need strength to fight many conflicting emotions. Just as an athlete has to fuel his or her body in order to perform, so must a practicing Christian fuel his or her soul in order to meet the spiritual challenges to which and through which Jesus leads us. It won't be an easy journey, but it's not supposed to be. The goal is to have a life-changing walk with God.

What gives me the right to challenge you with such a journey? As a pastor, I've seen how unwillingness to forgive hurts people. I've also personally experienced the liberating power of forgiveness. There's no way a person will have peace in life if he or she cannot forgive. Trust me when I say I have wrestled. When I think of the people whom I've loved and who've hurt me, I can get sad. But I've discovered that the pain lasts only as long as my unwillingness to forgive. When I'm able to forgive, I feel okay, perhaps distanced from the other, but thankfully I no longer have any visceral reactions when I think about or talk to the person. I now know that all of us "... fall short of the glory of God." (Romans 3:23) Also, although some relationships aren't meant to last forever, I can appreciate the learning and growth that come from them.

Over the years, I've watched the members of my congregation grapple with the challenges of forgiveness. I've seen some amazing transformations and liberations. We're learning that if we want to move forward, we'd better let go of grudges. I've watched them slowly and reluctantly give the pain to God and then surge forward in their lives. I've witnessed some amazing healings.

Jesus didn't come to ignore our suffering. He came to free us from the barriers that keep us from Him. I'm hoping that when you look into the chasm and see yourself and the issue that even now brings tears to your eyes, you'll get to a place where you can at least say, "Maybe I'll forgive." Forgiveness, or the process of forgiveness, is *Introduction* no easy thing. It takes time. You'll need to ease yourself into the *idea* of forgiving, which comes long before the *act* of forgiving.

This journey of forgiveness will bring you face to face with God, in the sense that you'll have "eyes that see" and "ears that hear" what His divine will is. You'll become convicted of the importance of pleasing Him, and that conviction will begin to slowly turn you away from your flesh and toward your spirit, that all-important part of you that wants peace and deliverance.

This face-to-face encounter will be painful. It's easier to see yourself as you wish to be rather than how you really are. How many of us squint our eyes when looking in a mirror to blur the wrinkles or rolls of fat? As you read this book, no squinting will be allowed! You must go to the chasm with your eyes and heart wide open. Get a journal and write your thoughts down as they come to you. Your thoughts will ultimately lead you to prayers of forgiveness.

When you get to the chasm you'll ask, "Forgive *who?*" and Jesus will smooth your furrowed brow. Trust that He knows your anxiety. He knows your heart and the heart of the Father, and He earnestly wants a marriage of the two. He knows how much you hurt. He knows what happened and how often it happened. He knows it all.

He also knows that even if we don't believe it, we really "can do *every*thing through him who gives [us] strength." (Philippians 4: 13) Even forgive.

Chapter 1
Unlimited Forgiveness

"THEN PETER CAME TO JESUS AND ASKED, 'LORD, HOW MANY TIMES SHALL I
FORGIVE MY BROTHER WHEN HE SINS AGAINST ME? UP TO SEVEN TIMES?'
JESUS ANSWERED, 'I TELL YOU, NOT SEVEN TIMES, BUT SEVENTY-SEVEN
TIMES.'"

—MATTHEW 18:21–22

In a room full of young teens I asked the question, "If someone killed
your child, then asked you to take care of his child after his execu-
tion, would you do it?"

Imagine the responses. The kids looked at me as if I had lost
my mind, and frankly, the question did seem to indicate a loss of
rational thought. Not surprisingly, their answers were negative.

The question came to mind as I watched a movie on the
Lifetime channel in which this very scenario formed the plot. As I
watched I wondered if I would be able to do such a thing. If I said
yes and tried to do what I thought Jesus would want, how would I
be able to look at the seed of the one who had killed my only child?
If I said no, would I be jeopardizing my relationship with Jesus the
Christ? After all, we're supposed to imitate Him as well as obey His
commands. If I said no, which would be the natural impulse, what
would I be doing to my relationship with Him?

It was too much for me to think about, so I threw it to the
youth. It was too much for them as well. One young person said, "If
that's what Jesus requires, I don't know if I can ever be a good Christian."

Disturbingly, unlimited forgiveness is what God requires. He
required it in the Old Testament:

> "If you come across your enemy's ox or donkey wandering off, be
> sure to take it back to him." (Exodus 23:4)

"Do not gloat when your enemy falls; when he stumbles, do not let your heart rejoice." (Proverbs 24:17)

"If your enemy is hungry, give him food to eat; if he is thirsty, give him water to drink. In doing this, you will heap burning coals on his head, and the Lord will reward you." (Proverbs 25:21–22)

Forgive Who?

With the new covenant, God then passed the ball to His Son.

When I read those verses to the youth, one of them said curtly, "If that's the way to get rewarded, I'm out of luck." When I asked why, he said, "There are some people and some situations that are just unforgivable."

That sounds plausible, or at least human. Most people would say that the offenses of September 11, 2001, are unforgivable. Some Christians would actually say that the Lord would want us to exact justice, which can be a catchword for revenge. To lay back and do nothing projects to the world the wrong image—that we are a punk people, afraid to fight back. That's unacceptable for Americans. In this country, mothers and fathers teach their children not to let anyone walk over them. "If you let someone hit you once, they'll surely hit you again," my mother would say. That directive to fight back posed a peculiar dilemma once when a bully hit me hard. I had two choices: run home crying and get in trouble for not fighting back, or hit her back and get in trouble for fighting. I fought back.

That little scenario is forgivable, minor in the grand scheme of things. How about the young men who claim they were molested by priests? Is sexual molestation committed by those who serve God professionally a forgivable offense? Should it be? Should the parents be forgiven even though, when told about the abuse, they chose to believe the priests and not their sons? Does Jesus really expect that?

Should the parents of Elizabeth Smart forgive the man who kidnapped their teen daughter and kept her for nine months? Should the wife of Richard Ricci forgive the police and media who relentlessly made him out to be the kidnapper, though he was later vindicated? Should the sister of Ron Goldman, who was killed along with Nicole Brown Simpson, forgive O.J. Simpson?

Recently, a young woman in deep pain was on *Oprah*. When

she was little, her mother's boyfriend repeatedly
told her mother, but her mother chose to let the boyfr
their home even after he was convicted and jailed for the c
woman was having an unbelievable time dealing with the si
She hated her mother, rightfully so. I wondered if the young wom
should forgive her mother for not protecting her, and the boyfriend
for hurting her. Should such a man be forgiven, especially if he has
admitted his guilt by apology?

Should mothers who desert their children be forgiven? Should
mothers who molest their children be forgiven? Should child abus-
ing, alcoholic mothers be forgiven because alcoholism is now called
an illness? Should Dave Pelzer, whose mother was unbelievably cruel
to him, even to the point of starving him, forgive his mother? More
importantly, *does Jesus expect him to?* Does Jesus really require forgiveness on all fronts? The scriptures would seem to say yes.

You see, forgiveness is not for the offender. Forgiveness is an
exercise for the one who has been offended. Perpetrators of pain in
your life may never feel or know the impact of what they've done.
If we spend too much time agonizing over their offenses, we don't
have enough room in our spirits for the healing power of God. The
healing power of God seems to be the only thing that can remove the
desire for revenge that we all have, or have had, from time to time.
Without God taking up residence in the sore and pained parts of our
spirits, we become hell-bent on finding ways to hurt the offender
as we've been hurt. I don't like soap operas, but they do dramatize
the quest for revenge that's so characteristic of us humans. There's
no room for the healing power of God primarily because there's no
desire for it. What we want is revenge, by our own hand or by an act
of God.

Have you noticed that acts of revenge don't seem to work—for
the most part? Taking revenge is like taking a drug; for a moment
one feels relief, a stupor, a high, a break or release from reality. One
may even smile and go to sleep, dreaming about the perpetrator "getting his" (or hers).

Eventually you have to wake up from that high, and when you
do, the high is gone but the pain is still there. Instead of being liberated, you're bound by a driving desire to make sure the person hurts.

he desired affect, i.e., the person hasn't
t is on to exact pain and suffering. Can
e spend their whole lives on such a quest

e us feel good, but only for a moment.
risoned by our pain, and that pain keeps
ce of God, which transcends understand-

oman whose only child had been killed by
was incredible. Not only had her son been
the memory that while she was pregnant
n hit by a drunk driver. As a result, the boy
had been in and out of hospitals throughout his young life. He had
finally gotten to a point in his life where his pain had abated; he had
finished high school, had gotten employed and was engaged to be
married. Everything was looking up for him. And then he was killed
by someone who decided he could beat the odds and drive drunk.

For a long while, the mother was trapped by grief, pain, and
anger. She wanted to see the "murderer" of her son "burn in hell."
Never mind that he cried during the trial. Never mind that he said he
was sorry. It didn't matter, she screamed inside. Her baby was dead.

Still, despite her pain, this grieving mother couldn't shake
the feeling that she should talk to the man. God was leading her to
talk to him. In the middle of the night not long after this man was
sentenced, she woke her husband and said she needed to go talk to
the driver.

She couldn't explain why she needed to talk to the man. She
only knew that she was "open to whatever God was going to do." God
surely knew her pain. She had railed against God and the man for
more than a year. Every time she looked at her dead son's picture and
realized she would never see him again, the tirades would start again.
She didn't want to live that way. Her husband understood, a little. He
felt like she was justified, which she was, in having her tirades. But
she began to sense that God was talking to her. She told her husband
she had to obey God.

She visited the man, not once, but several times. Strangely, disturbingly, she discovered that her anger began to dissipate. She didn't

4

want it to. What about her justifiable anger and pain? In spite of herself, she began to have some compassion for the man, and this felt like a betrayal of her son. How could she even be in the same space with this man? She felt guilty, yet different. Something was happening inside her. She wasn't feeling as bad as she had been.

One day she was surprised to discover that she had forgiven him. It made her mad at first. "Being mad at him, seeking revenge, made me feel in control," she said. "This feeling of forgiveness was not my doing." She fought it, even while she asked God to release her from her pain.

Unlimited Forgiveness

Because the pain had lingered so long, she thought God hadn't heard her prayers. Turns out He had been listening all along. The gradual release of her pain was, she realized, God working in her. She was experiencing Emmanuel or "God with us."

The day that she actually said to him "I forgive you" was a profound one for her. She began the day in tears, knowing she was going to visit him, but not really understanding what was going on inside her. When she visited him, she felt none of the familiar tightness that usually accompanied these visits. During the course of the conversation, she said it: "I forgive you."

When she finally forgave him, she felt a variety of emotions. A little anger. A little guilt. A whole lot of surprise. But the best were feelings of release and closure. She hadn't felt this way at the gravesite, during the trial and sentencing, or even when she'd learned from him exactly what had happened that horrible day.

Closure occurred when she let go of her need to seek "justice" (a.k.a. revenge) and let God do what God does.

She cried, and she noticed he was crying, too. That surprised her. Was that what Proverbs 25:21–22 referred to as "burning coals" being heaped on her enemy's head? Were his tears the result of the searing power of forgiveness? And were her tears a manifestation of the toxic emotions that were being purged out of her? Whatever. It was a powerful moment. She realized she no longer had to expend the energy to hate him and to want him to hurt. His fate was not in her hands, and she felt strangely free.

Her son's murder was surely what one would call an unforgivable offense, and yet, forgiveness was given. The divine part of that woman's spirit took over and a miracle took place. This is exactly what forgiveness of the so-called unforgivable is: a sure miracle and a miracle cure for the sick at heart.

᠔᠔᠔᠔᠔

Forgive Who?   Many of us confuse the terms justice and revenge. Some Christians would argue that Jesus allows justice, that Jesus would not expect us to sit by and do nothing if a horrible offense was done to us.

So where was the justice in the crucifixion? Who was rightly punished for the unjustified murder of Jesus the Christ? Who "got" the Pharisees, Sadducees, scribes, and other fickle folks who only a week earlier had praised Jesus as the Messiah? Who "got" Pilate for letting the unjust murder take place? I'm sorry. I must have missed it. I've never seen where justice, as we would define it, was done.

When people talked about (and still talk about) September 11, they say they want justice. When families want the murderers of their loved ones to be executed, they say they want justice. This definition of justice comes out of Hammurabi's Code that states, "an eye for an eye and a tooth for a tooth." That same mandate also appears in the Bible. Exodus 21:23–25 says, "But if there is serious injury, you are to take life for life, tooth for tooth, hand for hand, foot for foot, burn for burn, wound for wound, bruise for bruise." It's biblical, some would argue, for us to seek justice.

We don't understand that Hammurabi's Code, also known as the *Lex Talionis,* was not intended to promote vengeance. It was supposedly a tool of mercy to limit vengeance. Prior to its inception, vendettas and blood feuds were characteristic of society. If one individual of a tribe, for instance, injured another person, cultural mores allowed the *entire tribe* of the wounded party to attack the entire tribe of the offender. The *Lex Talionis* sought to limit this kind of tribal vengeance, which tended to knock out large lumps of society.

Another intent of this law was to prohibit an individual from exacting justice or vengeance against another person. The law was explicit in laying down the belief that it was the duty and responsibility of a *judge* to seek the justice. (Deuteronomy 19:18–21)

6

Finally, the law was almost never carried out literally. Jewish jurists argued that to do so might represent a miscarriage of justice, because in trying to "get even," a person might do more harm to his offender than was done to him. Judges sought to exact justice on five counts: a person was liable for damages done because of 1) the injury; 2) the pain caused by the injury; 3) loss of time; 4) loss of dignity, and 5) time required for healing.

Clearly, we have been confused about the "eye for an eye" statements. Moreover, we have ignored the fact that the Bible also says:

"It is mine to avenge; I will repay. In due time their foot will slip; their day of disaster is near and their doom rushes upon them." (Deuteronomy 32:35)

"The Lord is a jealous and avenging God; the Lord takes vengeance." (Nahum 1:2A)

[Jesus says,] "And when you stand praying, if you hold anything against anyone, forgive him, so that your Father in heaven may forgive you your sins." (Mark 11:25)

Christians have often used the Bible selectively to justify our points of view. We get strangely particular when we seek biblical justification of revenge or "justice." What's the difference between revenge and justice? Justice is not Hammurabi's Code or Exodus 21. In a layman's understanding, the Code and the biblical passage say, "Let me get you the same way you got me. Let me hurt you like you hurt me." That isn't the correct understanding but how, through the passage of time, we have adulterated the meaning of these directives. That's not justice. That's revenge.

My teen class discussed Jesus' response to society's misuse of Exodus 21:

"You have heard that it was said, 'Eye for eye, and tooth for tooth.' But I tell you, Do not resist an evil person. If someone strikes you on the right cheek, turn to him the other also." (Matthew 5:38–39)

They came to understand that Jesus didn't mean that you simply let yourself become a punching bag. "Turning the other cheek," said one young man, "means that you walk away and don't worry about someone thinking you're a chump. It means that you trust God to take care of you."

Justice is the appropriate retribution for a committed offense, and it's always administered by life. In my community we say, "What goes around comes around." There are spiritual laws in effect, which guarantee that justice will be done. God's laws are so much more precise and exact than human endeavor. The universe demands balance and justice, and God sees to it.

Our problem is patience. Justice often comes too slowly for us—in God's time, not ours. Those of us who are serious about our Christian walk need to know the difference between *kairos* and *chronos*. *Chronos* is the Greek root from which our word "chronological" comes and denotes human time. Our clocks keep human time, be it Pacific Standard, Eastern, Mountain, or Central Time. Chronos is measurable, and we find comfort in its precision.

Kairos is God's time, and truthfully, it's usually painfully slow and/or inconvenient to our human minds and emotions. What is God thinking about when He works on our behalf? Why in the world, for example, did He cause Mary, the mother of Jesus, to get pregnant *before* the engagement, causing Joseph to doubt her loyalty to him? God's time is slow and inconvenient. When we're hurting or angry, we don't have time for divine delay. We want justice and we want it NOW. We want to see the buster hurt who ruined our lives. We want to see him or her cry and suffer like we did. Never mind about God's time. We want a chronologically timed punishment, thank you very much.

But justice doesn't come in *chronos* time. It comes in *kairos*, God's time. Unfortunately, God isn't worried about what we want to see. He is only interested in what His wayward children need to learn. Only He knows at what hour His child will be ready and able to receive and learn from life's lessons.

Well, that's not acceptable to us. How many divorcees have wanted to see their husbands' or wives' new marriages fall apart? How many betrayed business partners have wanted to see their for-

8

mer partner fail? How many kids have wanted an unfair teacher to be fired?

We're not interested in *kairos*. Since we don't appreciate or respect *kairos*, we reframe justice in the human mold. Too often we go past venting about the wrong done to us and seek revenge, but call it justice.

Revenge is a drug. It's the crack cocaine of the Christian life. God doesn't dispense drugs. A person can't be liberated if he or she depends on drugs for relief and release. God gives freedom. Justice, applied by God, gives us release from pain. Justice doesn't mean we'll see someone hurt like we were hurt. Justice means that we'll feel the release to move on with our lives. We'll know that whatever God is planning for the one who wronged us will be done. We don't have to worry about it. The release that God gives those who truly seek justice is amazing. Justice is like a re-attaching to God after we've been violently snatched away. Justice is peace in the midst of the storm, where our enemies can see us but can no longer hurt us or even affect us.

Unlimited Forgiveness

Who wants to be addicted to something that provides only temporary relief? If I, as an African American, were intent on seeking revenge against white people for the wrongs done to us as a people over time, I would have overdosed by now. No, I don't want to be addicted. I want to be free.

Justice—letting God take care of God's issues—sets us free. Revenge, or the desire for it, keeps us trapped and has the power to make us do things we might not normally do.

Recently, there was a story of a professional, college-educated woman who discovered that her husband was cheating on her. She was mad, hurt, and humiliated. So she hired a private detective to follow her husband and his lover. She learned where they would be eating and decided to meet them there.

When they emerged from the restaurant, this college-educated, professional woman drove her Mercedes Benz full steam ahead and hit her husband. He fell, wounded. Not yet satisfied, she supposedly backed her car over him, though she denies that she did, and if she did, she says it was a mistake. To make sure her act of revenge was complete, she ran over him again. To add horror to this already horrible story, the man's 16-year-old daughter by a previous relationship was in the car when all this happened!

This previously sane woman decided to give the quest for revenge the upper hand! She was in so much pain that she lost her composure. Revenge said, "He should hurt like he has hurt you," and she listened to that voice. Now, the husband is dead, and the woman has ruined her life and the lives of her children. That's the way revenge works, unfortunately. It doesn't free us. It imprisons us emotionally, psychologically, spiritually, and sometimes physically.

What then? Forgive him? Forgive the husband who cheats? Is that what Jesus would say? Jesus would probably ask us, "What's the alternative? Would you rather be free or captive to your emotions?" Jesus leaves the choice to us, and if we choose to be captive, well, then, He allows us. But I think it makes Him sad.

We began this chapter with Peter asking Jesus how often we have to forgive. Do we have to do it once? Or is it something that has to happen again and again?

We have to practice forgiveness for as long as we live—hence, "seventy times seven" or "seventy-seven times." (Matthew 18:22) Why? Because as long as we are alive, things are going to happen that wound us deeply. Unjust situations, anger, and resentment will try and hold us captive. We're all God's children, but we all have issues. People and their issues will hurt us, and we, with our own issues, will hurt others. Forgiveness, and the practice of it, is a life-long proposition.

Does forgiving someone mean that we have to let someone hurt us over and over? No. To forgive is not to be stupid or masochistic. There's a story about a man who saw a wounded snake on the side of the road. The snake called out for help and the man had compassion on it and took it home and nursed it to health. One day, the man put the snake in his pocket and took it outside, and before he knew it, he felt a sharp pain. When he looked down, he noticed that the snake had bitten him. Hurt, he asked, "Why did you bite me after all I've

Forgive Who?

10

done for you?" The snake smiled and said softly, "You knew I was a snake when you picked me up."

Forgiving the one who hurt you doesn't mean you make him or her your best friend. It doesn't mean that you have to invite him or her over for tea and crumpets. Forgiveness simply means you allow God to heal your wounded heart and spirit. In the process, you'll begin to see that person as God's child, too. Forgiveness moves you out of the way so that God can do the chastising and correcting. Forgiveness means that you give yourself the ability to receive peace in the midst of the storm. *Unlimited Forgiveness*

Todd Beamer's widow Lisa was asked if she could forgive the men who hijacked United Flight 93 on September 11. She paused and said something like, "Well, I don't think I want to sit down with Osama Bin Laden, but what I do want to do is just be a good mother to my children."

It sounded like a "letting go" statement, like Lisa is trusting that God knows her pain and will take care of her and her children as He has thus far.

If we can accept the idea that God truly does take care of His children, perhaps we can get in the groove of forgiving "seventy-seven times"—in other words, practicing unlimited forgiveness.

Questions for Study

1. Are you harboring an unforgiving spirit? For how long have you been harboring it? Describe the origin of the hurt. Why are you still in pain? How long have you felt like this?

2. Do you put more credence in Exodus 21:23–25 or in Jesus' command to forgive? Why?

3. Is there a place in your life for practicing what the Exodus passage says?

4. What, in your mind, is the difference between justice and revenge?

5. Can a person seeking revenge ever be happy?

6. Do you want to enter into the process of forgiveness? Do you think it's possible? Why or why not?

Chapter 2
Too Angry to Forgive!

"THE DAYS OF MOURNING FOR MY FATHER ARE NEAR; THEN I WILL KILL MY BROTHER JACOB."

—GENESIS 27:41

Esau certainly had reason to be angry. His younger brother Jacob had stolen his father's blessing, and it could not be retrieved. His own flesh and blood had stolen what was rightfully his, and Esau was mad. It's one thing for a stranger to work against you, but it's quite another when someone you know, worse, someone you love and whom you presume loves you, works against you. Esau's resulting anger drove him across the thin line between love and hate, even to murderous intentions.

From the very beginning, there was trouble with Rebekah's boys. During her pregnancy, they even fought within her womb:

"The babies jostled each other within her, and she said, "Why is this happening to me?" (Genesis 25:22)

God told Rebekah that the boys represented two peoples (two nations) and that one would be stronger than the other. God said that the elder would serve the younger, which had to be disconcerting to Rebekah because that wasn't the normal way of life in ancient biblical times. When we think of this conversation between Rebekah and God, it makes it a little easier to understand some of Rebekah's actions later.

We can only imagine what Rebekah's labor must have been like, but when the boys were born, Jacob came out literally grabbing his older brother's heel. Talk about sibling rivalry! (Genesis 25:26)

The Bible says that father Isaac "loved Esau, but Rebekah loved Jacob." (Genesis 25:28) That must have been painful for Esau. It was good that his dad loved him, but face it: there's nothing like a mother's love. A mother's love is more understanding, nurturing, and kind, while a father's love prepares children for the real world. Two loves, equal in power but different in spirit. Every child needs both. When a child doesn't feel his or her mother's love, the pain can be unbearable.

One day, Isaac, old and approaching death, called Esau and said, "Prepare me the kind of tasty food I like and bring it to me to eat, so that I may give you my blessing before I die." (Genesis 27:4)

As Esau listened to his father, he had no idea that Rebekah was listening as well. With the words of God echoing in her spirit, 'the elder son will serve the younger," she decided to help God out to make sure God's words came to pass. As Esau scurried to do his father's bidding, Rebekah ran to Jacob and told him to get two young goats so that *she* could prepare food for his father. "Then take it to your father to eat, so that he may give you his blessing before he dies." (Genesis 27:10)

Jacob protested that Isaac, though old, knew his sons. "But my brother is a hairy man and I am a man with smooth skin. What if my father touches me? I would appear to be tricking him and would bring down a curse on myself rather than a blessing." (Genesis 27:11–12)

But Rebekah was relentless. She said she'd take any curse upon herself. So Jacob fetched the goats, and Rebekah prepared the stew. Before Esau returned with his bowl of stew, the deception was in full gear. Rebekah and Jacob succeeded in tricking Isaac, and the blessing that should have been Esau's was passed on to Jacob. It was a done deal. Once given, a blessing could not be taken back.

When Esau returned with his stew, he said to Isaac, "My father, sit up and eat some of my game, so that you may give me your blessing." (Genesis 27:31)

To Esau's surprise, Isaac asked, "Who are you?" Esau answered that he was in fact Esau, Isaac's first born. Trembling, Isaac said that he'd already been fed and that the blessing had already been given. The wronged son must have burned with rage. He didn't want to look at Jacob and Rebekah, but he couldn't help himself. Both of them stood there, Jacob probably looking frightened while Rebekah looked guilty or maybe even a bit smug. Esau couldn't believe it. The favored son had stolen what was his. (Genesis 27:32FF)

Playing favorites among children never works in families, and some of the scars from this practice never go away. The feeling of being rejected or unloved always seems front and center, even in adulthood. Some kids and adults act out because of their unresolved resentment of siblings who received more love, attention, presents, or whatever than they did. Children measure their self-worth by the amount of love they receive from their parents and by comparing this love to "how much" their siblings receive. For example, it's a no-no to spend more money on one than the other because, for sure, the one who receives less will know! In some homes, all siblings receive presents on each birthday to prevent the perception that one sibling is getting more attention, love, or things than another.

Clearly, favoritism isn't a good thing, but it certainly existed in the home of Isaac and Rebekah and now it had come to a head. There was no love lost between Esau and Jacob, and the relationship between Esau and his mother may have been damaged beyond repair (except for the saving grace of forgiveness). The pain of his mother's rejection! He was angry at Jacob but in pain over his mother's betrayal. Even if she preferred Jacob, how could she have stooped so low as to deceive her own husband?

Isaac told the distraught Esau that he had given his younger brother authority over him. Esau made one last, desperate attempt to change his father's mind. He said, "Do you have only one blessing, my father? Bless me too, my father! Then Esau wept aloud." (Genesis 27:38) But it was too late. The blessing had been given away, and Esau was out of luck. This story is so profound because it shows how an angry, unforgiving spirit keeps us miserable.

Esau was angry. He should have known Jacob would have been up to something. His brother had a deceptive streak a mile long. His mother, who didn't care about him anyway, had really hurt him this time. Could things get any worse? And then he remembered—not only did Jacob now have Isaac's blessing, he owned Esau's birthright as well. The blessing had been stolen from him, but the birthright—he'd given it away! (If only we could go back in time and undo our mistakes!)

This birthright transfer had happened not so long ago. Jacob was cooking some stew and Esau came in from hunting. He was hungry and asked for some of the stew. "Jacob replied, 'First, sell me your birthright.' 'Look, I am about to die,' Esau said. 'What good is a birthright to me?'" (Genesis 25:29-32)

Esau's answer was interesting and puzzling. Why would Esau say such a thing? Was he about to die because of some situation he faced as a hunter? Did the prospect of death plague him so consistently that he carried a fatalistic spirit? Did hunters expect to die sooner than most, maybe like corrections officers and firefighters expect death in present-day society? Or did Esau feel worthless because of his brother's more esteemed position in the family? Did that feeling cloud his vision and judgment and adversely affect his decisions?

The birthright was no small thing Esau was about to give away. In biblical times, a birthright, an inheritance of prosperity and name, was automatically given to the eldest or first-born son. The birthright was not earned; it was simply given. Although birthrights could be taken away, i.e., Reuben's birthright was given to the sons of Joseph (1 Chronicles 5:1), this was unusual because the family line was continued through the first-born son. The kingdom was given to the first born as his birthright. (2 Chronicles 21:3) Likewise, God made Israel His first born (Exodus 4:22–23). Paul had the privilege of Roman citizenship as his birthright. Esau and Jacob were twins, but Esau was born first and therefore had the birthright.

So, hungry or not, Esau should never have given his birthright away. Maybe he was so angry and pessimistic in general that he couldn't see the blessings he had in his life in spite of having a dysfunctional family. Maybe he was so used to being looked over that he didn't want to claim his place in the family. At any rate, he gave his birthright to Jacob for a plate of stew.

Anger can cloud our thinking, and Esau's mind and spirit must have been dulled by anger to have given away such a precious gift. Otherwise, he'd have heeded his spirit's warning to watch out for his younger brother, especially when discussing important issues. Mindless anger clearly affected Esau's ability to think clearly and act rationally. It's likely that Esau never even acknowledged his anger. He pushed the anger deep within him where it festered and caused him to live in resentment.

In order to be healed and enter into the process of forgiveness, one has to acknowledge the anger. Then comes forgiveness. We get confused sometimes. We think that forgiveness is tip-toeing through the tulips and acting like it's alright that someone hurt us. Jesus doesn't ask us to do that. It's not necessary to pretend that everything is alright when clearly it's not. In fact, denial is detrimental to one's spiritual health. It's all right, and even necessary, to get on our knees and admit to God that we're straight out mad. All of us who call on God in anger will find that anger converted to divine power. Rest assured, God knows your situation. God will work it out. Keizer writes, "The definition of forgiveness has something to do with the cessation of anger."[1] It's okay to admit to God that we don't understand what happened and why. It's okay to say to God that we really think He could have done more to prevent our situation and, therefore, our pain. Doing so is an important first step in entering the process of forgiveness.

Taking that first step isn't easy, no matter how much you may believe in forgiveness. Some years ago, a group of my deacons left my church. Led by the head deacon, apparently they'd been plotting and planning for months, and I'd been clueless. The fact that they represented my leadership was painful in and of itself; the fact that the head deacon was one whom I considered a surrogate mother just added salt to the wound. She said that she was leaving to do prison ministry, but I learned that what she'd actually done was lay the groundwork to begin a new church. When they left, I was angry and hurt; when I learned the depth and scope of their plan, my anger increased.

For the longest time, I pretended that it didn't hurt as badly as it did and that I wasn't as angry as I was. I wouldn't even allow myself to entertain unkind thoughts when I thought of the situation. I knew my congregation was watching me to see how I would act. I preached forgiveness all the time, and now I was being watched to see if I would put my money where my mouth was.

One day during prayer, however, I could no longer pretend that everything was alright. In the privacy of my prayer space, I railed against God and the deacons who left. How *dare* they do that to me and this church? How *dare* they plot and scheme while they were serving under me?!! How *dare* they (here was the real stuff I had to get out) embarrass me like that?!!

I was so angry, so mad. It wasn't fair. It wasn't right. Did I forgive them, in spite of all of my phony efforts? No way! In that moment of honest prayer, I had to admit—rather, God made me admit—that I wasn't anywhere close to forgiving them. I wanted them to hurt. I wanted them to pay for how they had hurt and taken advantage of me, or so I felt.

Honestly, I don't know what kinds of decisions or non-decisions I made during that period of intense anger. I don't even know how my sermons sounded because in the heat of anger, my spirit was covered by a cloud, which in turn clouded everything I said and did.

Shortly after I admitted my anger and asked God to forgive *me* for not being willing to forgive them, He began working on me. I resisted at first, but I really wanted a cleansed soul, so I kept at it. One day at altar call, I actually prayed out loud by name for those against whom I had held such anger. It surprised me so much that I almost stopped praying. Later, I wondered why God had orchestrated the process of forgiveness like that.

The next day, I knew why. You see, forgiveness is necessary because it frees us to do God's work. An angry spirit will hold us back every time. The next day, I received a call that the son of one of my members had been fatally injured in a work accident. As I rushed to the member's house, God whispered to me that a person whom I had named in prayer would be at the house. Of course this was true. This person, one of my former deacons, was the best friend of my grieving member. Lo and behold, the *first* person I saw, in fact, was this woman for whom I had prayed out loud the day before. For a moment, I felt the pain, anger, and resentment well up. I wanted to turn around, but the Lord said, "No. You're a step ahead of where you were." Concentrating on that promise, I went inside.

I felt okay! I was able to hug my former deacon and not feel any angst. I could move forward with the work I was called to do.

Had I not acknowledged the anger, however, and gone through the first cleansing stages of the forgiveness process, I would never have been able to even visit that home, much less sit in the same room with one who'd hurt me.

Anger is a natural response to betrayals, deceptions, and lies. Only forgiveness is powerful enough to deal with anger. Acknowledgement of anger makes room for the process of forgiveness to begin. Garrett Keizer writes, "Anger in the face of injury is a mechanism for survival, no less than the clotting of our blood."[2]

Anger isn't bad. It's normal and as Christians, we shouldn't chastise ourselves for feeling it. So for goodness sake, don't pretend that anger doesn't exist!

On the other hand, we can't let anger run the show if we want to do the will of God. Anger prevents us from wanting to do God's will in painful situations. If we as a nation spend too much time feeding our anger against the terrorists that changed our lives forever on September 11, 2001, we're going to shrivel up and die. Acknowledged anger is the beginning of power; redirected anger, or anger converted to positive action, leads us to the will of God. We witness God's power in our lives when our anger is redirected and channeled into good. This testimony of God's ability to replace our torture with peace and forgiveness will bless others as they see the change take place in us. Surely, such a change in our spirits, despite the wrong done to us, speaks well of the God we serve and of the things He demands.

❧❧❧❧

Before we move forward, perhaps we ought to examine why we're willing to hold onto anger despite the fact that it is so spiritually destructive. I mean, we do have a choice. I could have remained angry at my deacons. After all, they hurt me very badly. But I didn't want to go down like that. When we hold onto anger, we give our power to the ones with whom we have an issue. That, to me, was totally unacceptable. I don't want the "powers and principalities" to have control over me. I know that the fight is a hard one, but I don't want to give the power of evil a reason to gloat over another conquest.

Aside from the spiritual consequences of holding onto anger, there are also physical repercussions. Anger makes us physically sick. Studies have shown that anger stresses us out, raises our blood pressure, causes our immune systems to break down, making us vulnerable to disease, and produces unhealthy secretions in our bodies. Who knows how many cases of terminal cancer were exacerbated by anger that simply ate away at the insides? Once when I was in an unhealthy relationship and was angry too often, I prayed for God to give me the strength to end the relationship so that my health would not be affected. I pray all the time for God to be present in me so that His spirit will override those human emotions that might make me hold onto things that are not healthy for me. Unresolved anger and an unforgiving spirit are spiritual toxins that can kill us. They're like old food stored in a refrigerator. How often have you found, as you've cleaned your refrigerator, a forgotten bowl of food covered with black, white, or green fuzz, representing harmful bacteria? Despite having been placed in a space that was supposed to keep the food safe, that safety lasted only so long.

So it is with our anger. We bury our hurt, pain, and anger in "safe" places in our spirits so as not to disturb these difficult emotions. Often, we nurture them for too long. Anger is meant to be stored only temporarily, long enough to give us time to get it out. If we don't get it out, it rots inside us and gets covered with fuzzy stuff that poisons our spirits and our physical health.

Even if you don't buy what I just said, surely you must admit that anger makes us feel bad. It's the kind of bad that tightens up our gut, neck, and shoulders, and gives us a headache, takes our appetites, and makes us eat too much.

So why do we hold onto anger? Let me offer at least two reasons. The first is, we're afraid to let it go. The sad reality is that some of us are so used to feeling bad that we've elected to stay in that dark space. When the Israelites were being led through the wilderness to freedom, they wailed and whined as they traversed the unknown. When things got difficult, they grumbled and wished that they had remained in Egypt and left to die. (Exodus 14:12) They were treated horribly in Egypt, yet when the journey through the wilderness became too difficult, they openly yearned for their old, familiar pain!

It's scary to move toward deliverance. It's uncharted territory for us, and the journey is not without its difficulties. There are highs and lows, rocky terrain as well as smooth. We don't have a map. God has it, and He doesn't share with us the roads we must travel. So we travel toward deliverance with our hands in His, trusting Him, or at least needing to, and frankly, it's scary. We know our "hurting territory" very well. We know what to expect. We've even mastered our responses to our pain. What if, in the deliverance from our pain, we are faced with situations we know nothing about and feel ill-equipped to handle? It's too scary.

That kind of fear is the same kind that keeps a person in a job or situation that he or she hates. God says, "Let go. Trust me. Leave this job or this person and trust me to see you through." But we get used to suffering and become complacent. Rather than take the risks that will lead to a new life, we stay cooped up in situations that steal our joy and peace. We're afraid, and this fear keeps us rooted in anger when we should be seeking a release from it.

A second reason we don't seek release from anger is because being angry at someone or something gives us a sense of control. As long as we can point the finger at something or someone and blame it/him/her for our pain, we control the scenario. We can make someone feel bad for our pain. We can get others to rally against an unfair job or boss. We don't have to take responsibility for what we feel. It's someone else's fault, and everyone can see that we have just cause to be angry. The need to be in control is one of our most damaging human flaws. Bottom line: we would rather be in control than be free.

The alternative to God's release from anger is to rot like a corpse, even while we are alive. The story of Betty Broderick, seen on the Lifetime channel, showed this to be true. In the movie depiction of her life, Betty Broderick was married to a prominent attorney, but their marriage was not healthy. It seemed that Ms. Broderick was jealous, insecure, and prone to violent outbursts. Though her husband tried to please her, Betty was never contented. In one particular scene, the husband had given Betty a bracelet for Christmas, but because it wasn't what she wanted, she threw it at him, made a scene in front of her children, and stormed out of the room.

Meanwhile, the husband had a secretary who appreciated her boss and who provided a gentle alternative to his wife's violent personality. When one day Mr. Broderick came home to find chocolate icing (from a cake baked by the secretary for one of their kid's birthdays) smeared all over his bedroom and clothes, the final straw had hit the camel's back, and the husband filed for divorce. (Up until that point they were separated, but the husband had hoped the marriage would survive.)

Needless to say, that drove Betty over the edge, but the way the movie was done, it was almost impossible to drum up any sympathy for her. Her anger made her unattractive as a person. She would stop at nothing to make sure her anger was known to her husband and his secretary, who would later become his new wife. She would leave countless vile messages on his answering machine, swearing badly though she knew her own children would possibly hear her tirades. She was depicted as a bitter, demented, unhappy, and resentful woman who couldn't put the needs of her children above her rage. I didn't like her. I watch that movie every time it comes on, and every time I'm even more convinced that we must ask God to help us release from anger, lest we rot away inside.

The person who acknowledges anger and moves into the process of forgiveness isn't a wimp. The person who gives in to anger and lets it control him or her is actually demonstrating weakness. It takes strength, courage and hard work to let go of anger and then to willingly enter into the process of forgiveness. It's a spiritual exercise that's so painful most of us would rather not deal with it. At this writing, I'm training for a marathon, and every day, there's a point at which my muscles burn almost unbearably. I acknowledge that it hurts and the pain seems to make stopping justifiable. If I can run past the burn, though, I get to a higher level of ability. I'm able to run longer the next day, and the pain is less.

That's how it is with acknowledging anger *and* moving into the process of forgiveness. Acknowledging the anger is only the first step. We have to pray past the burn in order to enter into the process of forgiveness and move to the next spiritual level. If we don't, we limit our possibilities of spiritual growth and development. Once I railed at God about my anger and pain relating to my deacons, I felt a release. I knew that I'd be able to see and speak to any of them and move on. I dismantled one of the powers and authorities spoken of in Ephesians 6:12 that could have soured me for the rest of my life. I was able to look on that situation as a blessing as opposed to a curse, and as a result, I've grown. Even being able to acknowledge the experience as a blessing represents growth, thank God. He took me to the "next level" of spiritual maturity because of my willingness to enter into the process of forgiveness.

I'm not sure if Esau was willing to consider forgiving his brother. Angry and resentful, holding a grudge so powerful that it made him want to kill Jacob, Esau was a miserable human being. Some would say Esau was right to want to kill or at least hurt Jacob because the deceit was wrong! Esau wanted "justice," and some would say he was justified.

Ah, but we forget that justice comes from God, not humans. Esau wasn't seeking justice. He wanted revenge for wrongs done to him. He wanted to get back at Jacob for what he had done to him. He wanted Jacob to hurt like he was hurting. He was angry and wanted Jacob to know it and feel it. Anger clouded his spirit and his vision.

Ultimately, in this story, God worked out his justice with Jacob. Sometime after the deception, Jacob met and wanted to marry a lovely young woman named Rachel. In a perfect "what goes around comes around" scenario, Jacob was deceived by Laban, Rachel's father, and ended up marrying her sister Leah instead. In order to get Rachel, Jacob had to work for Laban for 14 years. Only God could have worked out a situation, which would so perfectly remind Jacob of his own deception toward his brother years earlier. Jacob felt the pain of being deceived in a way that Esau could never have conceived on his own.

In divine justice, God makes the perpetrator come face to face with himself. In the process, we learn about God's magnificent gift of grace. I'm always amazed at the story of Sir John Newton, the writer of the song "Amazing Grace." The story goes that Sir John, a slave trader, was overcome with a life changing revelation one evening while transporting slaves from Africa to the New World. He realized, from the "gentle whisper" of God, that what he was doing was wrong. No human being had been able to get to him like that. No abolitionist diatribe, no sermon, or stories, or physical evidence of the horror of the slave trade had touched him. Only God was finally able to reach him with His amazing gentle whisper.

After this encounter with God, Sir John was convicted of his sin. He was so moved that he wrote the words, "Amazing grace, how sweet the sound, that saved a wretch like me! I once was lost, but now am found, was blind, but now I see!"

How very true.

Questions for Study

1. Why do you think Esau gave away his birthright? Would you attribute it to anger or some other emotion? In the heat of anger, have you ever done something totally irrational?
2. Do Christians really want to enter into the process of forgiveness, or are we more comfortable holding on to our anger? Why do we hold on to anger?
3. Do you think Christians are afraid to pray honest prayers in which they admit their anger at a person, a situation, or even at God? Why are we afraid?
4. What do you stand to lose and to gain if you let go of your anger?
5. What does forgiveness do to help develop your spiritual maturity?

Chapter 3
Grudges, Grace, and Forgiveness

"When Rachel saw that she was not bearing Jacob any children, she became jealous of her sister."

—Genesis 30:1a

As we walk with God, He teaches us that grudges and grace cannot occupy the same space. In God's world, holding a grudge against another cancels out His grace—and His grace can demolish a grudge.

Grudges and grace are polar opposites. Grudges push us away from God and closer to our base human instincts. Grace, as a spiritual ideal, lifts us up closer to God. To be filled with grace is to be liberated from the emotions that normally keep us down.

Keizer writes that "If forgiveness is divine then it is not an act of willpower but an operation of grace."[1] He's absolutely correct. We cannot will ourselves to forgive someone. It has to be inspired, directed, and orchestrated by God.

God's grace is a mystery that we may never fully understand, but simply defined, grace is a free gift that we can't earn. But why do we need it, and why does God give it away so freely to us?

With grace we are empowered to perform superhuman acts, such as forgiving, which by ourselves we couldn't do. Grace allows us to be in God's presence. It lifts us toward God and enables us to seek and do His will, no matter how difficult. On one level, Jesus, who absolves us of our shortcomings, represents God's grace and His gift of eternal life. Had not God graced us by sending us Jesus, our sins would have led to certain death. (Romans 6:23) But just because God graced us with eternal life doesn't mean we're worthy; we still sin and fall short of the glory of God. (Romans 3:23) God's grace gives us some of that spirit, that divine substance that enables us to get over our human frailties that often prevent us from forgiving others.

Grace comes from God, but grudges come from the bowels of

our souls. A grudge is a "deep-seated feeling of resentment or rancor provoked by some incident or situation."[2] When we're consumed with a grudge, we're prevented from even seeking grace, much less experiencing it. While grace is a divine intervention into the human world, a grudge is a base, human response to the human world. Grudges turn us away from God and His will.

A grudge will hold us in bondage to negative emotions. While in this state of bondage, spiritual energy that could be used to get us closer to God instead fuels the grudge and keeps it alive.

In a recent Bible class, I asked my students to define a grudge. One of the best answers was that a grudge is a "hurt that you will not let go of."

"Can't or won't let go?" I asked. If we can't let go of a grudge, then it's beyond our control. If we won't let go of a grudge, then we're making a choice to remember the offense and to nurture negative emotions.

The class finally decided that both answers were right: sometimes we can't let go of the hurt, but most times we don't want to let go of it.

"Why would we want to hold onto something that makes us feel so badly?" I asked.

A student said, "Because we're not satisfied that the other person really knows how badly he or she hurt us."

"I understand," I said. "You're saying we want revenge."

"Yes indeed," said the student.

That was a disturbing thought. A grudge is a wound held in our innermost being, caused by someone we probably trusted and loved. Grudges are characterized by resentment, discontent, and "uneasiness in one's conscience."[3]

When we're in physical pain, we'll do anything to get rid of it: take aspirin or something stronger. After surgery, we take strong narcotics to ease the pain. Athletes take medication on the sidelines to get rid of the pain so that they can continue to play.

God has given us His grace to heal our emotional pain. Why do we *choose* to hold onto grudges? My students suggested that we hold onto grudges to protect ourselves from being hurt again. It's a defensive move, designed to keep us safe. Or so we think.

Sometimes we want to let go of the grudge but can't because the issue that caused the hurt was never resolved. To resolve the hurt, the "victim" has to feel like the "perpetrator" finally has *understanding, caring,* and *empathy* about the situation. If the victim can't exhale and say, "Okay, I think you get it," then the issue is not resolved and the grudge grows deeper. The seed of resentment that was already present in the victim begins to grow, and every time he or she is in the mere presence of the perpetrator, the pain is nurtured, because the soul hasn't been placated. Usually, the soul is closed to the idea that anything from God will help. The wounded soul pushes grace away.

To understand this concept better, consider how fear and faith work in our lives. If we have fear, we can't also have faith; if we have faith, fear is pushed out of the way. "And without faith it is impossible to please God." (Hebrews 11:6) Many of us are not pleasing God because we live in fear and not faith.

Fear of what? Mostly we fear that God is not all powerful. We fear that God can't handle our issues, pain, and needs. We want to believe, for sure. But face it. We believe that God is *up there* somewhere, and we, well, we live in the trenches. Since we can't physically touch God, we doubt that He really understands our dilemmas. We live with the ideas of what is both possible and impossible; we would submit that He does not. We read journals and newspapers. We study history and hopefully learn from what has happened in similar past situations. That knowledge doesn't keep bad things from happening again, and when they do, we wonder where God could possibly be.

We feel like God doesn't understand our predicaments. God doesn't have to balance a checkbook that has no money. He doesn't have to beat the odds in fighting a terminal disease. God doesn't have to go through the horrid pain of divorce and separation from a loved one. He doesn't have to bury children or parents and then "get back to normal." No, God's divinity puts Him on another level, one to which we are not privy. We say that there's no reason for God to entertain doubt and fear, and that maybe things won't work out the way He wants. God is God. He has it made.

I'm sure God understands our human complaints and rationales for being afraid. But if God could get our attention, I think He would ask us some hard questions like, "How can you say you believe in me when you don't believe in my power?" or, "How can you say you believe in me when it's clear you believe in yourself and what you can see quite a bit more?" The questions are sobering.

We'd counter His questions with some of our own. We'd remind Him that in hard times, we've looked for Him and expected Him to show up *in the exact way we requested,* and He did not. What then, we would ask, would He expect? How would He expect—how *could* He expect—us not to have some doubts when in all seriousness, His track record has been questionable at times? How would He expect us not to be afraid when we're called to walk on water and believe that drowning is impossible—although physical reality argues against the miraculous?

He'd say that fear cancels out the power of faith. When Peter became afraid, he began to drown.

It's crazy to believe like that, some would say. Absolutely nuts. Some might even argue that God wouldn't want us to believe like that. That's blind faith, and surely the good Lord didn't give us a brain capable of making brilliant decisions just to let it dissipate into a blubbering, believing mass of mush.

I saw that opinion written all over the face of a doctor who was attending to a child who had a brain tumor. All medical evidence said that nothing more could be done, the child would die, and soon.

The father of the child kept saying, "No, the Lord can heal her," and you could see the mixture of pity and contempt that clouded the doctor's eyes. He treated it as Christian gibberish, not even worthy of comment. The father refused to give into the fear that maybe the doctor was right. Although his little girl was gravely ill, suffering seizures and lapses of consciousness, her father held onto the belief that God was in control.

The little girl lingered, much to the surprise of not only the doctor, but the entire staff. The father continued to pray. That's what walking on water is, praying and believing, despite the fact that the water beneath you is really deep and you can't swim! The little girl came out of the coma. She sat up, ate, smiled, and talked. The doctor was amazed, and although the little girl did eventually transition into the arms of Jesus, the doctor had been touched. He reminded me of the centurion who stood at the foot of the cross and said, "Surely, this man was the son of God!" (Matthew 27:54) The day before the little girl died, the doctor said with misty eyes, "I've been taught. Truly, your faith in God is greater than the medical odds that are against this little girl."

God holds the water beneath our feet and allows us to experience the impossible. When Peter got out of the boat on the Sea of Galilee and started to walk on the water, he didn't sink. As long as he kept the vision of Jesus before him, he was alright.

But, as will happen when we take our eyes off Jesus, fear gripped Peter. *"When he saw the wind, he was afraid."* (Matthew 14: 30) Peter began to sink. In the same way, when we take our eyes off God, we lose His grace. We give into base human instincts and become subject to those emotions. When Rachel began to hold a grudge against Leah because Leah could bear children and she could not, she pushed grace away as the grudge took up residence within her. With the grudge driving her, she persuaded her husband to sleep with Bilhah, her maidservant. (Genesis 30:3) The union produced one son. If Rachel had not been consumed with resentment of Leah, would she have conceived such a scheme? She condoned a second mating between Bilhah and Jacob and had another surrogate son. Even with two sons, the enmity between Rachel and Leah still existed.

Leah, too, held a grudge against Rachel because Jacob actually wanted Rachel and not her. Time passed and Leah had many children, a fact that should have made her happy. But she couldn't forget that Jacob had slept with her because of a mistake, and so she held a grudge against her sister. When Rachel wanted some mandrake plants that Leah's son Reuben was bringing to her, Leah tersely asked her sister, "Wasn't it enough that you took away my husband? Will you take my son's mandrakes, too?" (Genesis 30:15)

Maybe somewhere deep inside, Leah knew she was being petty. It wasn't as though there was a scarcity of mandrakes; there were enough to share. But the grudge she held against her sister was stronger than the grace that would have allowed her to share the mandrakes and move on. Holding grudges makes us forget the grace that God has given us. It makes us forget the blessings we already have.

Consider Leah, who, though not the favored daughter, had been blessed by God with four sons! The grudge pushed the memory of God's goodness far away. As Leah held onto her grudge, she couldn't forgive Rachel for her status as favored daughter. Rachel's grudge against Leah blocked God's grace from healing her spirit.

Holding grudges prevents our spirits from receiving the grace needed to forgive. Our spirits will push grace right out of the picture, just like fear pushes faith to the curb. If we want to forgive or enter into the process of forgiveness, we must realize that the grudge has to go, right here and right now.

Grudges, Grace, and Forgiveness

≈≈≈≈

My children were planting pumpkins and flowers in the backyard of our newly leased house. I was happy because we seemed settled. Since my divorce, we had moved three times in as many years, and I was tired. This felt like it would be the last move for a while, and I was glad.

On the other hand, I was furious with my ex-husband and his new wife, whom he had married less than a year after we divorced. They had been as smug as bugs in a rug in the great big Victorian home I had left when we separated. They never had to incur any moving expenses, not one time. Not only that, but even if they did have to move, they could have easily afforded it. With the two of them working well-paying jobs, they were comfortable and had been since my marriage broke up.

I was mad. I resented my ex-husband for cutting me off of his health insurance, not helping me pay our children's daycare tuition, and not offering to help with the daily extra expenses for the children. I was struggling to make sure that their quality of life didn't slip, and couldn't understand why he wouldn't help.

I was mad at him and mad at *her*. I was mad because she had so easily moved into *my* territory. I knew they'd been seeing each other before we separated. I resented her, too, because she seemed so *perfect* for him. I knew I hadn't been like she was. I'd been too independent, too selfish, too opinionated. In my quiet moments, I knew all of that. The knowledge didn't stop me from resenting her, though.

Anyway, I thought I was working through it. I'd been praying about it. I'd gotten over wanting to do something to him to make him hurt, but I still resented him. I still held a deep grudge against him for hurting me so badly. That's all I thought about: how badly he had hurt *me*. I carried that hurt wherever I went. It came out in everything I did and in everything I preached. I didn't know how pervasive my pain was.

Then one day my children and I were planting pumpkins. I'd gotten into planting stuff because *he* had been into it and the children liked it. So, as we planted chrysanthemums, impatiens, and other flowers, and pumpkins my son Charlie said, "Mommy, can we invite Dad over to help us?"

I wanted to die. *Invite him to my house? Are you crazy?* There was no place in my heart or spirit to be kind to him. I'd been polite, but kind? No. And polite was pushing it.

I was all set to say no and give him some lame excuse why, but then the Lord made me look into my son's eyes. Did my grudge against his father justify keeping the two of them apart? The human part of me didn't want his father to come, but the spiritual part of me had another idea. As I stood there looking at Charlie, tears filled my eyes because I knew that a crack had been made in the grudge and now grace could slip in. I realized the words of scripture were true: "But if … you seek the Lord your God, you will find him if you look for him with all of your heart and with all of your soul." (Deuteronomy 4:29)

Through my pain, I'd been seeking God and asking Him to change my heart. I'd been praying for God to loose me from the anger and resentment I felt so that I could move on. I didn't want to damage my children or my congregation with my unhealthy emotions. At that moment, I knew that my seeking God was paying off.

Honestly, I wasn't completely happy with the revelation, but I was relieved. I was relieved because I could actually *feel* the power of God pushing my "stuff" to the side. It was a remarkable moment. I was able to say to Charlie, "Okay, he can come."

We got on the phone and invited him. He sounded incredulous (as was I in this demonstration of God's power). He paused and then agreed to come over. The children were happy, and I was fine. I was amazed, but I was fine. God had given me that elusive peace, and I knew it. (Philippians 4:7) I didn't feel one iota of anger, fear, or resentment. I should add that he later called and said he couldn't come because his wife didn't think it was a good idea, but I was at peace. The grudge had begun to dissipate because grace was finally doing its work.

What made that event possible was my prayer, despite the pain, for God to have His way. I didn't want to be a hypocrite to my congregation or my children. Plus, I *needed* to know if God could really work when the pain is that deep.

Grudges, Grace, and Forgiveness

What I learned is that God not only works to dissipate our pain, He also shows us how we participate in these situations, either as victim, perpetrator, or both. He works on the parts of us that have been victimized, but He also shows us how we've been perpetrators as well.

God brought me face to face with myself and the situations in which I'd been the perpetrator. Sure, my ex-husband had hurt me, but I had hurt him, too. That's the power of grace and how it leads to forgiveness. In my struggle to get rid of the grudge I held against my ex-husband, God had to show me that I hadn't been Miss Goody Two Shoes.

Even now when I think about it I want to protest. I didn't leave him. I didn't fool around. I didn't refuse to help him raise the children. I didn't marry within a year of being divorced. God acknowledged that, but He also showed me how I'd hurt him, too, and I have had to come to terms with that. God made me remember things I'd done and said and how my ex-husband must have felt.

For example, God reminded me of how, on his birthday, which was also the day I was ordained into the Christian ministry, I forgot to wish him happy birthday. His mother had to remind me to say something. I'd been so wrapped up in receiving all the attention that I neglected to say something that was pretty important. When God reminded me of my neglect, I couldn't believe I'd been that selfish.

That's what grace does. It breaks up the crust that surrounds grudges. It won't let us point the finger too long, and it reminds us that we've been forgiven ourselves for some pretty heinous, selfish, thoughtless acts. As we've expected and desired forgiveness for ourselves—and received it—we must likewise forgive others. Grace says that we cannot be content to rest in our victimization. Grace simply won't allow that.

What is it that keeps us perpetrators (for we've all been perpetrators) from admitting that we messed up and really hurt someone? What do we feel we're losing, or would lose, by "fessing up" and offering an olive branch? What are we holding onto? What are we trying to protect to the exclusion of those whom we love?

"I think it's pride," offered one friend. "It's not easy to admit that you were a complete ass." Nicely put. It isn't easy, but the price of not confessing our sins is immense. How many of us are still holding grudges against our parents? Are our children holding grudges against *us* because we insist on being *right,* even at their expense?

Parents have a hard time apologizing. We've got to learn how to say, "I'm sorry" or "I was wrong."

On an *Oprah* show a while ago, Dr. Phil attempted to help a mother say, "I'm sorry" to her two daughters. The daughters resented (held a grudge) against their mother because her mate had sexually molested the girls when they were young. The girls had told their mother, but she hadn't believed them. When it became obvious that they were telling the truth, the man was arrested and served time. But when he got out of jail, the mom *let him back into the house.*

The girls hated her for it. One of the sisters had worked through her pain, but the other was not even close. Dr. Phil tried to help the mother mend her relationship with her daughters, to resolve this issue that held them all captive.

Mom needed to be able to say, "I'm sorry. I was wrong." But she absolutely could not do it. She couldn't admit responsibility for anything that had happened. She kept offering excuses, justifying her actions or non-actions. She presented *herself* as the misunderstood victim. She couldn't relate to or understand her daughters' pain. In fact, she was angry that the daughters didn't understand *her* situation.

The segment left me in tears because I could see what was needed, as could Dr. Phil, Oprah, and millions of viewers. But since the mother couldn't see it, her daughters left the program probably more wounded than before the program began. The grudge may have become greater, not less.

It's not difficult to understand that we, the grudge-holders, must atone for what we've done. As much as we don't want to admit it, there's someone out there who was victimized by something we said or did. It's hard for a human spirit to accept the divine task of admitting weakness. So we stubbornly hold onto being right at the expense of others we've wounded. We brood because we cannot or will not atone and admit our culpability. Atoning for our actions could be the first step toward healing someone else. Our failure to admit that we've hurt someone else is yet another way we keep grace at bay.

In the meantime, we, the victims, continue to hold the hurt inside, incubating it and feeding it more tidbits of memory, resentment, anger, bitterness, and other choice toxins. When we incubate a grudge by constantly reliving the offense, grace is kept out of the picture. A victim's sense of self-righteousness can keep grace away as effectively as a perpetrator's failure to admit wrongdoing.

Is it any wonder that grace is the antithesis to holding a grudge? Grudges imprison us, but grace *frees* us. With grudges, we want the other party to experience pain so that we can feel justified and vindicated; with grace, we decide to let God handle it. With grace, it's no longer important for a person to suffer because he or she hurt us. We no longer worry about making sure that the perpetrator "gets his." We don't have to figure out a way to make the person hurt. We're free! And we realize that being free is more important than being right or getting revenge.

The fact that it takes us so long to accept grace, maybe even invite grace to scour our souls, means that we have a serious relationship problem with God. One of the reasons we hold onto a grudge, is that we're not convinced that God knows, understands, or can deal with our pain. While it may be good spiritual jargon to say "let go and let God," we're not willing to do that. It's inconceivable that an invisible God who lives far away from us would have a *clue* as to what we need to feel better.

Indeed, the Biblical directives show that God is out of touch:

"Do not seek revenge or bear a grudge against one of your people, but love your neighbor as yourself. I am the LORD."
(Leviticus 19:18)

"Do not say, 'I'll pay you back for this wrong!' Wait for the Lord, and he will deliver you." (Proverbs 20:22)

Forgive Who?

"Do not say, 'I'll do to him as he has done to me; I'll pay that man back for what he did.'" (Proverbs 24:29)

Forgiveness truly is about letting go and letting God. Holding onto a grudge means we don't trust God. If we really trusted God, we'd know that He can keep us above the waters that threaten to drown us. We'd know that He knows more about His game plan than we do. When we trust God, that means we want Him more than we want grief, freedom more than we want the bondage to our pain.

Trusting God means that we accept the grace that frees us and helps us to trust Him more.

❧❧❧

What do we say to someone who is nurturing a grudge? How do we remind him or her that God cares about feelings of intense anger and pain?

What could we have said to Esau? That he shouldn't feel anger against his brother? No, that wouldn't do. He had a right to the pain. The injury to his soul was real.

Would we tell Leah or Rachel that "God never puts more on you than you can bear?" Would that have helped Rachel as she watched Leah bear son after son or Leah, knowing that her husband preferred her sister over her? They'd need time to lick their wounds then get to a place emotionally where they could even *think* about God. When we've been hurt, we're not inclined to jump up and down and celebrate the presence, love, or justice of God. In fact, when the big hurts come, we're angry with God for letting it all happen. We question whether God really is all good and all-powerful. If so, then why would he allow the hurt to come? When pain is inflicted, we tend to get very mad at God for allowing the situation to happen.

Would reminding Leah and Rachel of their relationship as sisters have helped? I don't think so. These women had done too much to hurt each other.

Can't you hear Leah? "Rachel didn't seem so concerned about honoring the sister-thing when she took Jacob. As beautiful as she is, she could have gotten anyone she wanted. But no, she wanted *my* husband."

Can't you hear Rachel say, "How can I honor Leah as my sister when she was constantly reminding me that I couldn't conceive? She knew how much I wanted to give Jacob children, but she just had to keep rubbing my nose in it."

I can hear them both asking, "Why should I care when Jacob didn't bother to honor our relationship?"

Actually, there is precious little an outsider can say. The willingness to let go of a grudge and reach for grace is a personal decision, a spiritual leap to a level of faith that's difficult to imagine. It's hard to make the leap because the victim has to hurdle not only feelings of disappointment, rage, anger, bitterness, and resentment, but also the feeling of being *disappointed with God* for letting it all happen. A person has to be willing to lay all his or her broken eggs on the table, then let go so that God can repair the cracks. At the time of deep spiritual hurt, few of us are willing, or able, to do that.

We as Christians too often think that because we join church and then eventually begin to listen to God through the scriptures that it should be an easy thing to drop our old ways. Even after praying and reading this book, you still might not be ready to enter into the process of forgiveness. It doesn't always happen that way.

Being a Christian is something you do. It's not something you are. Doing what Jesus asks of us sometimes takes years. I prayed for two years to be able to let go of my grudge against my ex-husband. I'm still praying after five years for the grudges I hold against my deacons to be fully erased. I saw one of the deacons once in an amusement park and felt my whole body tense up. I knew I wasn't healed, but that's the goal: to know where we are and how far away from the ideal of forgiveness we actually are. Our prayers must be earnest and

35

steady in order for the grudge to be penetrated. "Letting go and letting God" is no overnight event.

We have to get to the point where we can and will pray for our victims and our perpetrators. In so doing, we begin our own process of healing. James wisely wrote that "the effectual fervent prayer of a righteous man availeth much." (James 5:16, KJV) When the wound

is deep and pulsating, the injured is in need of divine care. We wouldn't expect a patient to heal his or her own disease. Likewise the emotional victim can't be expected to heal him or herself. Emergency care must come from the spiritual realm as an answer to our prayers. It's not that we're spiritually deficient. It's just that the pain is too great, and we need help. We're not always as strong as we'd like to think. Especially in intimate relationships, we're open and vulnerable. When we've been betrayed or hurt, the pain is so great that only the Great Physician can come to our aid. Praying for those who have hurt us seems to hurry His response time to us.

Left untreated, a physical injury—a stab, gunshot wound, broken bone, or hemorrhaging organ—can kill us, or at least leave us permanently maimed. So too, a spiritual wound left untreated can kill our spirits, hope, joy, and desire to live. The difference is one type of wound can be seen with the physical eye; the unseen wound can be publicly denied.

When someone we care about is struggling with a grudge, we must enter into prayer and "bear the infirmities of the weak." (Romans 15:1, KJV) When we do so, we have joined the Spiritual Emergency Trauma Staff as a care provider. If the wounded grudge-bearer is earnestly seeking God (and that may or may not be evident for some time), there will be a crack in his or her protective armor. One day, he or she won't be able to resist God's grace that begs to enter in and heal

Once the immediate trauma has passed, it's the responsibility of the wounded to take an active part in his or her own rehabilitation. Those who have sustained serious physical injuries know they must often endure painful therapy to get back to normal. If you've sustained a serious spiritual injury, the healing will come only if you take an earnest part in your own recovery.

Before The Great Pumpkin Incident, when my ex-husband was about to marry his second wife, a friend called me and told me o pray for him. I stared at the phone. Truly, this guy was crazy, and guess what? I wasn't going to do it! The audacity of such a suggestion just made me angrier.

But my friend was in the spiritual emergency room and was applying a retractor* to my resistant soul. I resisted at first, but I couldn't keep up the anger. I didn't want to give my power, joy, and future to a grudge! After a long time, I muttered a prayer, and I do mean muttered. That mutter represented the crack through which grace could pass. After a while, I found myself (in spite of myself) actually praying for his health and for the health of his new wife, the stepmother of my children. Is God awesome or what? Is grace magnificent or what? That first prayer chipped away at the grudge I held and made the pumpkin day possible.

Grudges, Grace, and Forgiveness

When my friend told me to pray for the father of my children, I needed help, and the help came from those who prayed for me as I lay incapacitated from emotional and spiritual pain.

I wish I could say I'll never be incapacitated from that kind of pain again, but I know I will. The power of grace, though, is that when it happens again, I'll be stronger. The grace I've received is like a tonic that is building my spiritual being. If I become incapacitated again from a pain, I'll be able to call on the reserve of grace I have inside in order to pray for the additional grace I'll need. I'll remember that letting go of the grudges in the past freed me up, and I'll be less reluctant to suffer silently with my spiritual pain. I'll know that being willing to enter into the process will begin to alleviate my pain. I'll know from past experiences that grace really does work. I'll know for a fact that "if any man be in Christ, he is a new creature: old things are passed away; behold, all things are become new." (2 Corinthians 5:17, KJV)

I want to be a new person. No more grudges. Just a lot more grace.

---

*A retractor is used in surgery to move the bones aside so that the surgeon can operate on the organs.

Questions for Study

1. Do you agree that grudges and grace cannot occupy the same space? Why or why not?

2. Are you holding a grudge against someone? For how long have you been carrying it?

3. What happened to cause the grudge? Share the experience with a support group or write in a journal the circumstances that brought you to where you are.

4. Are you unwilling or unable to let go of the grudge? Why? What do you have to gain by holding onto it?

5. Can you identify a time or times when you did something to hurt someone? Have you made atonement for what you did? Are you willing to?

6. Have you been able to identify the unresolved issues that are blocking your forgiveness of the one who hurt you? Have you shared those issues with the other party?

7. Are you admitting you have a grudge? Or are you hiding the bleeding wound pretending that it's not there?

8. Do you empathize with Leah or with Rachel? If you were in Jacob's situation, what would you do?

Chapter 4
Tea, Crumpets, and the Divine Directive

But I tell you, do not resist an evil person. If someone strikes you on the right cheek, turn to him the other also."

–Matthew 5:39

What did Jesus mean when He gave the divine directive to turn the other cheek? In the context of forgiveness, does it mean letting someone hurt us over and over?

As a child of the '60s, I watched the protestors of the civil rights movement practice what Jesus said to do. No matter how much the water hurt from the fire hoses or how vicious the dogs were, the people protested peacefully; they refused to fight back. Their nonviolent stance was admirable, and it was biblical. When at last some gains were made for African Americans, I took it as proof that turning the other cheek was a powerful tool to use against those who oppress or hurt us, socially and individually. Dr. King learned from Ghandi, who used the technique as well, and was able to actualize great changes for his people.

On an individual level, we can use this same tool in our practice of forgiveness, with some differences in purpose and application. In society, abuse will continue as long as we allow it, and it's the same on an individual level. Nonviolent resistance to social injustice is a mirror that allows oppressors, victims, and bystanders to search their souls and assess their actions. On a personal level, we may take the first "hit" but turn the other cheek in various ways that ensure our safety and jumpstart the process of forgiveness and grace.

Allowing continued abuse in the name of forgiveness represents a misunderstanding of the divine directive. We don't have to be martyrs in our relationships; Jesus took that hit for us on the cross. Turning the other cheek means that we don't fight fire with fire, and we certainly don't seek revenge. We forgive the person for having hurt us, but we don't have to invite him or her over for tea and crumpets! We're allowed to forgive and keep a safe distance for our own protection.

A friend and I argued about Jesus' divine directive. My friend couldn't understand why I'd even talk to someone who had done some pretty painful things to me. I said to my friend, "I forgive him. It's over now. I know who he is and what he's capable of, and it doesn't hurt me to talk to him."

Forgive Who?

"Humph!" my friend snorted. "I wouldn't even talk to him. I don't get it. You're setting yourself up to be hurt again."

Not so. The only way I'd be in danger of being hurt again by this other person is if I invited him into my *space,* the place in my being where I'm vulnerable. For the longest time, I'd invite him back and every time I'd become the subject of yet another act that hurt me I didn't get it; I had misinterpreted the divine directive. That space I speak of is my spiritual "home," and folk can come by invitation only!

When people hurt me, I withdraw my invitation—they can't come back into my heart or my house. Now that I understand the divine directive, this man can no longer sup with me. I won't fix him dinner or invite him for an afternoon of tea and crumpets to talk and share. From a distance, I can care about him and even help him if he needs it. I've gotten to this point because I've dropped the grudge and allowed grace to direct my path. But I cannot and will not invite him into my space to get burned again. I still talk to him on occasion, and can even laugh with him! I appreciate his strengths and am aware of his flaws. I won't give him an opportunity to bop me again because I won't let him that close, but if he ever needs help and I can give it, I'll do it. That's grace working.

The reality is that there are some people who have done us wrong once and will do us wrong again. Turning the other cheek doesn't mean we continue to let people hurt us. It simply means that we no longer hate, despise, or resent them for who they are and for what they've done. We've learned to let go of our pain, and we've moved on.

This is the same lesson many abused women and men need to learn. I often counsel abused Christian husbands and wives who are grappling with how to honor and obey the commandments of Jesus and their wedding vows while surviving in an abusive situation. I tell them that God doesn't want them to die for the sake of honoring wedding vows or the commandment to turn the other cheek. God doesn't want us to hurt for the rest of our lives; He's not that kind of God. In some cases, I've advised them to leave the relationship.

What God does require, though, is that they pray for and forgive their spouses for the pain they've inflicted! Being able to pray for one who has hurt you so deeply is a sure sign that one's connection to God is working and that grace within you has the upper hand. Physical, mental, and emotional abuse comes from deep issues within an individual that only good therapy and a life-changing relationship with God can treat. Most people who abuse others really don't like themselves and they hate what they do, yet, as written in Romans 7: 19, "For what I do is not the good I want to do; no, the evil I do not want to do — this I keep on doing."

So we're commanded to love them and forgive them. We just don't have to have them over for dinner.

We show that we misinterpret Jesus' divine directive by continually inviting people into our lives who shouldn't be there. It's as if we live in a constant state of denial. Though someone may have hurt us badly, we can't or won't believe he or she really *meant* to hurt us, or we think that in time he or she will change. We think, as we invite them again and again into our most vulnerable and intimate space—to a table of tea and crumpets that ought to be reserved for the most honored guests—that one day they'll appreciate the invitation and will honor it. Common sense and the voice of God intervene on occasion to get our attention and convince us that we're being foolhardy, but we don't listen. In the name of forgiveness, we make allowances that go way beyond what Jesus would expect of us.

We think we're honoring the command to forgive, but what we're really doing is honoring a need we have in *us*. That need might be to prove that we're not bad people. Too many of us grow up thinking we're bad and unworthy, and spend countless hours trying to prove to someone, anyone, that we really are *good people*. Some of us may even measure our "goodness" on the amount of abuse we can take and still stay on our feet. So we forgive the abuser—which is the right thing to do—but then we invite the abuser back into our space to do the same thing he or she did before, maybe with more intensity. We think they're hurting us because we deserve it, and we reason that we must forgive them because they're only doing what's right. We pray that they will forgive *us!*

Some of us will do anything, at the expense of our own happiness and spiritual growth, to get someone to like us. As a child, I'd buy things for people so that they'd like me, but my mother would always say that I couldn't buy their love. Well, that was just fine. How else was I going to get them to like me? They called me horrible names and teased me for being tall and skinny and a crybaby—except when I gave them something.

One day my mother sat next to me and asked, "How long are they nice to you after you buy them something?" I had to admit that their friendliness was always fleeting. "Forgiving them for being mean to you is okay," she said, "but you don't have to let them keep on hurting you." It took me a while to realize that just because they came to my birthday parties didn't mean they liked me. Instead of getting the mean ones to like me, my time was better spent honoring the ones who did like me and learning how to enjoy the rest of my time alone.

We may continually invite people into a space they don't need to be to prove to ourselves that we have the power to change another person. In the guise of forgiveness, we invite people over to "help" them, but the truth is, we just want to change them. That's probably not going to happen, no matter what we do or say! We have plans for how we'll act, how we'll respond to something this person has done in the past and is likely to do again, and if that plan doesn't work, we come up with another one. Seldom is God in the midst of any of these plans, and seldom do the plans work.

I've seen all kinds of people change, including drug addicts, prostitutes, liars, negative people, child abusers, and mean-spirited people. They didn't change because of another person's efforts. Only the intervention of God, and in some instances the maturity that only time and life experiences can bring, created true change. Now, if we're truly trying to help someone, not for our sake but theirs, we may grow spiritually strong with the effort, but that's not always the

42

case. Often, we're interfering with God's work. How long will it take to finally admit that change may not happen easily and that our best bet is to leave well enough alone? The answer depends on how close we allowed the person to become.

God allows us to continue the ill-advised invitations until we have taken all we can after there has been much pain and wasted time. Before us are half-empty cups of tea and crumpet crumbs, evidence of people who ate at our table but took our hospitality and kindness for granted. Apparently, God waits patiently for us to wipe the table clean and never extend that invitation again.

۞۞۞

Samson, the Nazirite, was a man honored by God but who often sublimated his relationship with God to his desires. He jeopardized his special status by hanging out with evil people. (Judges 14:1–3) Although a very spiritual man (Judges 13:25), at times he gave in to his carnal desires and appetites. (Judges 16:1) God gave him great physical strength (Judges 16:3), but he was weak when it came to resisting temptations. (Judges 16:15–17). In other words, he was a lot like us.

Samson's story is fascinating. His mother, nameless in the Bible, and his father, Manoah, had been childless for years. The story goes that one day an angel of the Lord visited the couple and told them that they would conceive and have a son. "No razor may be used on his head, because the boy is to be a Nazirite, set apart to God from birth, and he will begin the deliverance of Israel from the hands of the Philistines." (Judges 13:5) Samson's mother was advised not to drink any "wine or other fermented drink ... and not [to] eat anything unclean." (Judges 13:4) Manoah and his wife did as they were told, received confirmation of the conception from the Lord (Judges 13:18–21), and gave birth to Samson. From the beginning of his life, the Bible says "the spirit of the Lord began to stir him." (Judges 13:24–25)

Samson knew he was blessed, but he always had a weakness for women and their antics. Prior to his infamous meeting with Delilah, Samson met a young Philistine woman, and he liked her so much

43

that he wanted to marry her. He and his parents went to Timnah to make the marriage arrangements.

On the way there, Samson went off by himself. A lion approached him. The spirit of the Lord came upon him (Judges 14: 6), and Samson tore the animal apart with his bare hands. There was some honey on the carcass. He ate it and also gave some to his parents, although he didn't tell them where he got the honey. In fact, he didn't tell anyone about the lion or the honey. He decided to have some fun with his secret during the wedding feast, which lasted seven days.

Forgive Who?

Samson told a riddle to his new friends at the feast (thirty companions). He said, "If you can give me the answer within the seven days of the feast, I will give you thirty linen garments and thirty sets of clothes. If you can't tell me the answer, you must give me thirty linen garments and thirty sets of clothes." (Judges 14:12–13) He told them the riddle: "Out of the eater, something to eat; out of the strong, something sweet." (Judges 14:14)

For three days, the companions could not answer, and they began to pressure his wife to help them. "Coax your husband into explaining the riddle for us, or we will burn you and your father's household to death." (Judges 14:15) So, she bothered Samson for the answer until finally he gave in and told her. She explained the riddle to her people and Samson, in anger, "went down to Ashkelon, struck down thirty of their men, stripped them of their belongings and gave their clothes to those who had explained the riddle." (Judges 14:19)

It was Samson's weakness to give in to women.

So, it's not surprising that once again, he'd be seduced by a woman. This time, the woman was Delilah, and she was beautiful. Those who knew Samson and his weakness for women knew they had an opportunity to capture and conquer him. Up to this point, he'd been unstoppable. Filled with the power of God, he'd defeated the most formidable enemies. His would-be captors wanted him out of the picture, and when he fell in love with Delilah, they saw their chance.

"See if you can lure him into showing you the secret of his great strength and how we can overpower him so we may tie him up and subdue him," the Philistine rulers told Delilah. "Each of us will give you eleven hundred shekels of silver." (Judges 16:5)

44

Delilah began to work him, and here's where the tea and crumpets phenomenon kicked in.

Each night, Delilah would seduce Samson and ask him about the source of his strength, and each night, he'd tell her a different story. The following day, she'd test his story and his enemies would lie in wait, ready to take him captive. But it never worked. Samson had to have known that Delilah was working to undermine him.

Yet, each night, he'd invite her again into his space. They'd make love. She'd tell him some lie to smooth over his ruffled feelings, and then, when he was totally intoxicated with his feelings of lust, she'd try again to get him to share the source of his strength. He had to have known he was in a bad place. He had to have heard the voices of God and common sense telling him not to give in to his desires, but he was too weak. It was his need and lustful desire for her that drove him. Perhaps he thought his love for her would prove stronger than her deceptive nature. He needed her love, and it was this need that tied him to her. Night after night he'd invite her to a place of intimacy she didn't deserve.

Finally, after failing several times to discover his secret, she whined and complained so that she drove a spike into his emotions. 'How can you say 'I love you' when you won't confide in me? This is the third time you have made a fool of me and haven't told me the secret of your great strength … So he told her everything." (Judges 16:16–17) He offered her the ultimate invitation to tea and crumpets: access to his most vulnerable and private spiritual and emotional space.

The secret of Samson's strength was his hair. Remember, before his birth he was set aside as a Nazirite, and Nazirites never got their hair cut. God had given him a special dispensation. As his parents had obeyed God, so should Samson.

For the lust and desire of a woman, Samson revealed the source of his strength. The men in hiding swarmed Samson, cut his hair, and he lost his strength. As he looked at Delilah in the midst of the confusion he must have thought, "I trusted you. I knew you were lying to me, but I gave you chance after chance to be different. You said you loved me. I let you get closer to me than any woman." He remembered how he repeatedly invited her to tea and crumpets, but it had all been for naught. Samson was captured, and he died, even as he pushed against the columns of the temple so that a great number of his enemies were killed. His was a death that didn't have to be. If only he'd invited a worthier woman to tea and crumpets.

Turn the other cheek, for sure. Jesus meant that. But He doesn't require that we invite people to hurt us over and over. That stems from our personal needs, not the divine directive. Forgiving one's enemies and turning the other cheek might mean we get hit again but it shouldn't be from the same angle or for the same reason.

Forgiving someone doesn't mean you become his or her toy. Forgiving someone means you take that first hit, pray for the strength not to retaliate, and then walk away. Other hits may be levied against you, but you won't be affected by them because you've moved out of the strike range and are allowing God to handle it.

It would seem that the challenges before us are great. We must examine not only the divine directive, but the reasons we find ourselves in difficult situations. I've experienced peace since I've learned that forgiving people doesn't mean I have to let them abuse me, emotionally or otherwise. I no longer chastise myself for keeping certain people at bay, though I *harbor no grudge against them.* It's truly a feeling of liberation. It must be what Jesus wants us to feel.

Questions for Study

1. Who is it in your life that you keep inviting back into your space? Why do you do it? What are you getting from this relationship that you can't seem to let go of?

2. What's the difference between forgiving someone and letting him or her use you?

3. Up to this point, what has been your understanding of the divine directive to "turn the other cheek?"

4. In your journal, write down reasons that you've been unable or unwilling to turn the other cheek. Is it because you haven't understood fully what Jesus meant?

5. Could you see, from the story of Samson and Delilah, the pattern of human behavior that gets us into situations that make it hard to forgive?

6. Can you find another story in the Bible that illustrates either 1) the power inherent in turning the other cheek, or 2) the tragedy that comes from inviting people to tea and crumpets who don't deserve the invitation?

Tea, Crumpets,
and the
Divine
Directive

Chapter 5
Forget Not, Forgive Not

"But one thing I do: Forgetting what is behind and straining toward what is ahead, I press on toward the goal to win the prize for which God has called me heavenward in Christ Jesus."
—Philippians 3:13–14

My son Charlie is a very intelligent young man. He goes to school every day and seems to like it. But he has a most amazing ailment: he can never remember if he has homework, or if he does, what it is. Worse, if he did the assignment, he can't remember where he put it. Our nightly conversations go something like this:

"Charlie, do you have homework?"

"No, Mom."

"Are you sure?"

"I said no, Mom."

"Not in any class? Not math, not English?"

"Oh yeah, I think I have homework in math."

"What is it?"

"I don't know. I don't remember."

Charlie and I have that conversation often throughout the school year because I know he has a problem turning in his homework assignments. Still, when report cards come out, I'm always disappointed when the teacher, noting a less than favorable grade for my brilliant child, says, "He's so bright, Mrs. Smith, but he doesn't turn in his homework."

Every time I get that comment from a teacher, I see red. This is a kid who straight out tells me he doesn't have homework or that he turned it in. When I confront him after an irritating meeting with his teacher, he'll look at me and say, "Mom, I forget that I have homework." Or, worse, "Mom, I do it, but I forget to turn it in."

Come on! *I'm* the older one entitled to senior moments, not this 13-year-old kid. How can homework just slip his mind?

Actually, our lessons on forgiveness can shed light on this ability of the human mind to completely *forget* something that's unpleasant to us. Forgetfulness is absolutely necessary to experience the freedom of forgiveness. Some would say it isn't possible to forget the pain, and yet, we forget terrible pains in our lives all the time. I remember watching on television a woman giving birth to a child and declared, at the ripe age of 5, that I would never have children. My mother smiled, and said, "You don't remember the pain." I gazed again at the agonized woman on the television screen and wondered how my mother could say such a thing. Yet, there had to be something to it. She had five children. I knew of women who had even more children. I was still dubious about the truth of her pronouncement until I had my own children. Although the pain of childbirth can be beyond description, the joy of having my children shoved the memory of the pain aside.

Jesus aptly explained the mystery and the power of forgetting pain when He said, "I tell you the truth, you will weep and mourn while the world rejoices. You will grieve; but your grief will turn to joy. A woman giving birth to a child has pains because she knows her time has come; but when her baby is born, she forgets her anguish because of her joy that a child is born into the world." (John 16: 20–21) It's possible to forget one's pain when joy follows suffering.

Here's the catch: *the pain has to yield to a joy greater than the pain endured.* That sounds crazy, oxymoronic. It doesn't seem possible that we can experience joy when we've been hurt so badly. Mothers aren't the only ones who receive the gift of forgetfulness after the labor pains have ended. We all can experience joy and relief after we've pushed the painful emotional mass out of ourselves. Although we remember that something hurt us deeply, the joy will not allow our spirits to recall the specifics. It's like giving birth to a new spirit!

Recently, a member of my congregation came to see me. We've had some grave misunderstandings between us, but with time, we've both grown and come to an understanding. Anyway, she came to see me and finally asked, "I need to know how I hurt you. What did I do to hurt you?"

I paused, then replied, "I don't remember." I was telling the truth. When I looked at her, I remembered that I had hurt for sure, but I couldn't remember why, nor could I remember the depth of my pain. "I don't remember," I repeated. "It doesn't matter anymore. That was then, and now is now. All I know is that things are better now, and for that I'm grateful."

Out of pain had come the joy of forgetting.

Now when I say joy, I don't mean that we experience happiness and feel the "warm fuzzies" toward someone, although that's possible. The joy I'm speaking of is the *relief from having to support and feed the pain*. Joy is the gift given to us when we allow grace to do its work.

We may not forget everything, nor does forgetfulness come easily. In the above example, I entered into intentional prayer, asking God to help me release my anger and pain. But sometimes, if I'm hurting too much, I don't ask God for help. It's as though I won't let myself forget. I've learned that if I don't ask Him to help me release my anger and pain, I remain stuck in my emotions and I'm unable to feel the joy. Instead, I feel the ongoing pain, the acute aching when I meet my oppressor face to face or even when I just think about the situation. I feed the pain with memories and emotions to remind me of its legitimacy in my life. Being angry and hurt doesn't make sense. It's an exhausting experience that takes too much energy.

Is it possible to forget, even when someone has destroyed your life or murdered your child or loved one? It's possible, though difficult. One of the most powerful examples of forgetfulness and forgiveness is the case of Peter and Linda Biehl. Amy Biehl, their daughter, was on a Fulbright Scholarship in South Africa. In August 1993, two days before she was due to leave the country, Amy gave a ride to some South African friends and encountered a mob shouting anti-white slogans. In a brutal attack, Amy was stabbed to death.

In an instant, a loving, vibrant daughter was gone, but the Biehls said a remarkable thing. Peter Biehl said, "There was never any question about our position. It was a time for humility, a time for forgiveness."[1]

Amy had prepared her parents for such a catastrophe. She had told her parents that the black people in South Africa were angry and were doing to white people what they felt had been done to them for too long. She had told them that when black people died, it was as though they were insignificant and unimportant, with hardly any mention of what they had been about, while when white people died, they were given complete obituaries and much respect.

When Amy was murdered, her parents had a perspective that helped them deal with the murder. Still, no one would have blamed them for being bitter and angry. Murder is wrong, heinous, and wretched. Yet, the Biehls were able to sublimate their pain to their desire to carry out what they thought Amy would have wanted. They announced that they wouldn't oppose amnesty for the killers, and when asked if they weren't angry, they said that their willingness to forgive the killers was only right in a country where reconciliation and forgiveness is national policy. They later helped two of the four convicted killers start a business which transformed their community. Their backing came through the Amy Biehl Foundation, which has more than 300 employees in Cape Town.

Peter Biehl (now deceased) later said, "We grieve our loss, yet forgiveness has freed us."[2] He'd forgotten the need to hurt, and this enabled him to move beyond the pain of the past. It's a gift of grace to be able to do that.

God wants us all to experience the miracle of forgetting past hurts. He wants us to give birth to joy and to relish the beauty of that joy, "forgetting what is behind and stretching forward to the prize" that He has for us. Instead of living lives of misery, haunted and tormented by memories of what's been done to us, He wants us to see beyond the moment and into the space reserved for us when we allow grace to work. That means we'll forget about...

- wanting others to understand or care about our hurt feelings. Face it. Some people will never understand what we feel or why. It's a waste of time to try and get a reaction out of them. In fact, we deepen our anger. We'll feel relief only when we accept that we probably won't get the reaction we want from the person. When it's no longer important to make them understand why their offense hurt us so, the intensity of the pain lessens, and we begin to move on.

- getting a reaction from the offending party. As children, we went to great lengths to make sure the offending party knew how we felt. We wanted them to hurt like they hurt us. As we mature emotionally and spiritually, we no longer depend on reactions from others to determine how we feel about ourselves. We know that through God's grace, we can forgive, release the other person, and move on with or without their reactions to our pain.

- getting revenge. We'll never forgive or forget if revenge is our motive. In order for revenge to work, rage, pain, and disappointment must be fed all the time. As long as I wanted to get revenge on my ex-husband for leaving me, I was miserable. I didn't want to do anything to him necessarily, but I wanted some vindication for what he had done to me. I waited for a long time to see his demise, and when it didn't come, I wasn't happy. Not only that, I was mad at God! My ex-husband wasn't getting what he deserved. In fact, he'd been blessed with a new wife and a new life! As long as I wanted him to hurt, I was unhappy. When I reached the point where it didn't matter, I began to experience spiritual freedom. Only God can mete out punishment. When we really understand that, we're free.

- needing to be right. So many arguments develop into situations that cause great and lasting pain because of our need to be right. A friend of mine, commenting on a situation with his wife that was causing them some strife, said to me one day, "I had to decide whether I wanted to be married or right." The desire to be right closes our ears to the other person's point of view and sets us up as blameless. We become self-righteous and that's destructive to the forgiveness process. Even if you're right, sometimes it's better to just back away from the argument and the need to prove that you're right. This allows us to deepen our relationship with God. We are peaceful and free from the burden of feeling wronged.

- creating vows that lead us down roads even angels fear to tread. We endanger our spiritual well-being when we create all-consuming vows of revenge. To vow that a person will pay for what he or she has done sets you at odds with God. Jesus says, "Love your enemies and pray for those who persecute you, that you may be sons of your Father in heaven. He causes his sun to rise on the evil and the good, and sends rain on the righteous and the unrighteous." (Matthew 5:44–45)

We also make "I'll never" vows as a negative reaction to pain. For example, when hurt by love, we may say, "I'll never love again" or "I'll never trust again." Never say never because this type of vow could create a lifetime of pain, heartache, and loneliness. Negative vows take us out of God's will and grace, and that's a place where none of us wants to be.

When we receive the gift of forgetfulness, we free up space in our spirits for new messages, ideas, and feelings that say God is in control and our pain will be dealt with by Him. Our bodies respond differently, too, to this renewal of mind and spirit. Our emotions become lighter, and we're relieved of stomach cramps, headaches, high blood pressure, and other physical maladies. This relief comes from being treated by God. We become confident in the work of God and the Holy Spirit, and like the Biehls, we make something good come out of pain.

It's our call.

⋆⋆⋆

A woman once told me, "I forgive people, but I don't forget." She said that whenever she sees someone who hurt her in the past, she feels pain, anger, and the desire to just stay away.

She hasn't forgotten. Nor has she forgiven.

The human mind has the ability to forget unpleasantness, but it can also tenaciously hold onto painful thoughts. There have been times when I've made myself remember incidents that caused hurt or anger. For some strange reason, I wanted to hold onto my hurt feelings. I hate when I do that! Thank God for my stronger desire to practice and experience forgiveness.

When we deliberately hold onto mental pictures, feelings, and thoughts related to a painful incident, we tamper with the letting go process that forgiveness requires. We interfere with God's work of creating peace within us.

Recently, I purchased some shoes for my son and daughter. If you've ever bought clothes or shoes for a teenager without their input, you know this is unacceptable. At the time, I didn't realize that, so I purchased some sneakers for them both and was quite proud of my choices. Since my son loves skateboarding, I purchased a skateboard I found for a bargain.

Forgive Who?

Well, to put it mildly, they weren't impressed. Straight out, my son said, "I can't wear those!" He wasn't impressed with the skateboard either.

"What do you mean?" I asked, hurt. "I went out of my way to get you those shoes, and you're not even going to wear them?"

For the next couple of days, I pouted. My feelings were hurt and I wanted him to know, so I wore a sad face when I was around him and made remarks so that he would know that I was bothered. I wanted him to react, to care! I wanted him to put on the shoes that he hated to please me.

It wasn't going to happen. So, in a moment of self-pity, I said, "I'll give the shoes away and never buy you anything again." He did not care. He was not upset. That made me angrier, made my hurt feelings bleed all the more. But it didn't matter. I gave away the shoes and skateboard, and he was happy.

I held a grudge for about a month. That's a lot of sore feelings to nurture. Then it dawned on me. Families break up over little stuff like this. No one can make me like something, nor can I, a parent, make my kids like things that they don't like. My best bet was to forget my pain and forget about the incident, learn the lesson I was supposed to learn, forgive my son for not reacting the way I wanted him to, forgive myself for holding a grudge, then *forget about it.*

Forgetting can be hard to do. It involves the effacement of the ego in order to make room for the transformative power of the Holy Spirit. It's the ego, after all, that gets in the way. The ego, fed by pride, is only concerned with what the self wants and needs. It's completely consumed with making the self feel better or right, at any expense. When my son rejected the shoes and skateboard, my ego and my pride were at work. Once I forgot my needs, I could forgive my son.

The inability to let go of painful memories is what keeps us from forgiving. We might as well face it: the water is over the dam or under the bridge; the situation is over. Holding onto painful memories means we *want* to stay in pain or we don't know we have a choice.

Some might argue that this explanation is too simplistic. We *want* to stay in pain? No way. But the truth is, we can decide to follow a different course. If holding onto painful memories is making us feel bad, then we can decide to let go of the memories. Letting go may be as difficult as trying to lose weight. Making the decision is only the first step. Taking action is the next step and is often difficult. When the desire to change, however, overshadows the desire to remain the same, there's a different fuel infusing our spiritual systems. The desire to change usually intensifies as we find ourselves experiencing small victories, and we push forward.

Continuing with the weight loss analogy, as the pounds start dropping off, we'll push to remain on course with the weight-loss plan in order to continue seeing success. It's the same way with forgetting bad memories. As time goes on and you remain dedicated to releasing pain, there will come a day when you'll forget to remember, forget to feel the hurt. You'll think, "Wow! That was a relief. I didn't think about it once all day!" That one day will become two days, then a month—and then there will come a time when you seldom ever think about the incident, and if you do, there's no strong emotion attached to the thought. As we see how forgetting bad memories frees us up, the more we'll want to continue the process.

Not looking back is an important part of that process. When I began training to run a marathon, sometimes I would look back to see how far I'd gone. As I progressed in the number of miles I was able to run, however, looking back was no longer something I wanted to do. I wanted to see ahead. I'd name landmarks I wanted to reach before I stopped to catch my breath. As long as I kept the goal ahead of me, I found I was able to run further and further. Spiritually, it works the same. When we look back, we hinder ourselves. We *see* again what bothered us so, and we can stumble and fall if we're not careful. Forgetting what's behind is absolutely necessary in order to really forge ahead.

The good news is that we're in control of what we feel. Nobody can make us feel anything we don't want to. By holding onto bad feelings, we give those feelings power. Forgetting means we orchestrate a spiritual shift and give power to feelings that lift us up and liberate us. No one can do anything about the fact that bad things happened to us when we were young. But we can decide what happens next. When we decide to forget the bad experiences, we release powerful spiritual enzymes that will break up the tumors of hatred, anger, bitterness, and resentment that have been sucking the life right out of us for far too long.

Forgetfulness is a choice. When practicing forgiveness, we must choose to forget.

Choosing to forget the hurtful things people have done to us is one of the most difficult decisions we'll ever make. I wish I could say that I've forgotten all the incidents that have caused me great pain over the years. There are some things I've been able to forget, and therefore, forgive, but there are other things that still cause me a visceral reaction. There are some people I'm not ready to forgive, which means I'm choosing to remember my pain.

It's my decision, and I realize that. Nobody is keeping me out of recovery but myself. But I can say this: when I work the process, the process works for me. The more I'm able to release and forget, the more liberated and peaceful I feel.

A while ago, I came face to face with a woman against whom I had held a grudge for something done to me some time back. As she approached, I paused for a second. It wasn't too late to make a turn so that we wouldn't have to meet. But I'd been praying for release for a long time and realized that I didn't need to run away. I had allowed God to excise my pain and apply the healing power of the Holy Spirit. I walked toward her.

To be honest, when she smiled at me, I wanted to vomit. Her smile seemed so phony. She held out her arms to hug me and I hugged her back, without emotion. To my surprise, I lost nothing in the exchange. What happened happened, and it was over. Thank God, I'd forgotten the depth of my previous pain, and it no longer crippled me. She no longer had the power to affect me. Once we'd been close, but now that things had changed, we could say hello, hug, and keep stepping. There would be no tea and crumpets. Her invitation to be a part of my life had been respectfully withdrawn. I'd forgiven her because I no longer needed her to hurt, and I was free.

That's the gift of forgetting.

I can hear the protests. Some might say that the pain they've experienced is too great to forget about. They may resent the suggestion that they should and want to forget. These protests are feelings and emotions-based, which are highly unreliable. Once, a woman, newly widowed, came to me in tears. I thought she was crying because she was feeling the loss of her husband. To the contrary, she was crying because she *didn't* feel badly and was afraid she was doing his memory a disservice.

"We loved the Lord, and we really prayed through his illness," she said. "He told me he was ready to see God, and I felt peace from that. When he died, I knew he was okay. I didn't feel bad then and I don't feel bad now." But she wanted to feel badly because she thought she was supposed to.

When dealing with someone who has offended us, we must remember not to depend on our feelings and emotions for reliable guidance. They're too vulnerable, and they will lead us astray. This is a spiritual journey, and we need the Holy Spirit to lead us in the right direction.

Beware of well-intentioned friends who may or may not be supportive emotionally. They may not understand your decision to forget and forgive. They'll feed your rage, sense of betrayal, and desire for revenge. They'll bring chips and dip to your pity party. Since we can't depend on other people or ourselves for this spiritual journey, let's depend on the Holy Spirit for inspiration and guidance. The Holy Spirit will assuage our spirits and raise the bar on our human behaviors. The Holy Spirit understands the divine nature of this forgiveness journey and will give us "living water" to keep going even when the journey seems too hard and our souls are parched with anguish. (John 4:13–14)

One other thing that might help in the process of forgetting and forgiving: when something bad happens to us, when we're hurt, betrayed, or wounded, realize that it's not necessarily a bad thing. Pain is a part of growing up. It allows us to become aware of what life is about—what hurts, why it hurts, and how to avoid that hurt in the future. Babies learn that stoves are hot by touching them and possibly getting burned. In the long run, the experience can be categorized as good because of the valuable lesson that was learned. Paul Brand and Philip Yancey write in *The Gift of Pain* that feeling pain is one of our greatest blessings. It lets us know when something is not good for us.

He says that lepers often lose fingers and toes because they can no longer feel the pain that comes from being burned or injured. By the time they become aware of injury, it's too late; irreparable damage has been done.[3] Pain is God's gift that keeps us from repeating the same mistakes over and over.

Sadly, some people just don't understand pain's teaching function. When I was little, I only had to get spanked one time for any given offense. My parents didn't have to scold me repeatedly for the same things. I hated spankings and I hated being put on punishment. Unfortunately, I was quite talented at finding new offenses for which a spanking or punishment could be given, but I never got spanked twice for the same thing. On the other hand, my sister was always getting in trouble for the same offenses. Her memory of the pain didn't outweigh her desire not to hurt. In the same way, many of us choose to satisfy our human whims over and over rather than ending the vicious cycle of pain and giving into temptation.

❧❧❧

Forgetting and forgiving don't mean that we're to condone what was done to us. If we forgive, we cease to feel resentment about a situation, a phenomenon which can only come if we agree to forget the importance of our pain. Condone means to "pardon or overlook voluntarily; to treat as if harmless or of no importance."[4] Forgiveness is not the same as condoning an offense. To forgive is to let go. We get confused and angry when we misunderstand what forgiveness means. Nobody, not even Jesus, requires us to condone the wrong done to us. Jesus didn't condone being crucified or wrongly accused by those who said they cared for him. He didn't condone Peter denying him, Judas betraying him, or even Thomas not recognizing him. He forgave them. He let their offenses go.

You can't condone being raped or molested, nor should you. You're not expected to condone the murder of your child. You don't have to condone the fact that your father or mother neglected you, lied to you, or abused you. That's not what forgiveness means.

Forgiveness means you let go of resentment and you forget about needing an emotional response from others.

My mother died after I graduated from high school. Although I was devastated, I was still expected to continue my education. All my life, my parents talked about the importance of education. It was drilled into us, and I studied hard to make sure I'd be eligible for someone's university.

My plans to go to college paused as we dealt with her death. When things calmed down, I presented my father with the paperwork he needed to fill out in order for me to receive financial aid. He refused to fill out the forms or help me with tuition, yet he said he expected me to attend college. This hurt my feelings more than I can say. It never occurred to me that my parents wouldn't help me out financially.

I was stunned. Without the papers, I wouldn't receive any money. How was I going to manage? I was so hurt. I cried a lot, and then I got angry. There was no way I was **not** going to college. The message to pursue higher education had been too much a part of my daily life. There was no way I was going to detour from the path now.

So, I got a job. On campus, off campus, both. I worked. I was angry, I was hurt, I was mad, and I resented my father. I had nothing to say to him.

When I was a junior, my feelings began to surface. They were debilitating. So, I began to seek a way out. I was in school in California; he lived in Detroit with his new wife. I began to write to him, honest letters, expressing how I felt and why. The more I wrote, the more I had to write. I didn't accuse him of anything. I simply rehearsed and reviewed what had happened between us that had caused me pain. As I wrote, I cried sometimes. Sometimes, I smiled because I was remembering *good* things in the midst of the bad. I don't know what he thought of those letters; we never discussed them. But at least he knew and could now share in the burden I had been carrying for too long.

When it was time to graduate, I sent my father an invitation, but I was devastated inside because I knew how he thought. I knew he wouldn't come. I was too far away, and he wouldn't pay the airfare. To appease myself and bandage my wounded spirit, I bought a "happy graduation" card, on which I signed his name and then mailed it to myself. That way, on graduation day, I could show that my dad cared enough to at least send the card.

Do I need to say again how angry I was? How much I resented him?

But the letters I wrote helped me. As time went on, I resented my father less. The Holy Spirit (though I didn't identify it as such then) was working on me, helping me to forget the pain I'd carried for so long and the desire for him to understand my pain. Slowly and surely, the pain dissipated until one day I realized there was no active throbbing left.

When my father was stricken with cancer some years later and was on his deathbed, I realized that the healing was complete. I'd forgotten enough to be able to accept him as he was. His neglect no longer mattered. I'd graduated and moved on with my life. (He had the audacity to be proud!) In fact, I was in graduate school and would soon graduate from there. My letting go had allowed me to move forward and to stop trying to extract from him something he couldn't give. As I stood there, looking at him in the casket, one of his closest friends came up beside me and said, "He loved you so much. He told me everything about what you were doing and how proud he was."

I was truly surprised. I never thought he paid much attention to me or what I did, nor did I think he cared. Later, my stepmother said that he had said to her that he never knew how to love children. He said all he knew was how to provide and discipline, so that's what he did, but he wished he'd been able to really love all of his children more.

Because I had released so much of my anger, I was able to receive the revelations. My brothers and sisters were still angry with him and I'm not sure how much better they felt, if at all, as they learned the ways our father had thought and operated. But I knew I'd grown. Because I'd been able to forget my pain, I could accept his weaknesses, which had so adversely affected me. I was able to accept him as a human being and to take him off the hook for not being what I had defined as a perfect or even good father. It no longer mattered to me what he hadn't done. I had forgotten, and this enabled me to forgive and be thankful for what he *had* done. I was liberated from the pull of my own messed up emotions.

If this sounds easy, it isn't. The day I wrote the first letter to my dad, explaining to him why I was hurt about so many things, I began to feel the liberation. It didn't matter if he responded or not (he did not); what mattered was that I was getting all that pain *out*.

My strategy was to write my father a letter, but that may not work for everyone. There are other things you can do to begin the process:

- Don't keep talking about the pain you're trying to forget. The more you talk about it, the more power you give to it. Talking about the situation is like pouring salt in a gaping wound. It doesn't lead to healing at all. When I stop talking about something painful and instead start praying about it, the process of forgetting and forgiving becomes easier. Each day I feel less angst about the issue than I did the day before.

- Don't try to get people on your side. When you talk about an experience to someone, you're really trying to justify your feelings and get troops on your side. I tell newly married couples NOT to talk to their families when problems arise because sides will be taken and the need to be right will be fed. The more you get people to justify your hurt, the deeper and more intense the pain becomes.

- Be honest with yourself about why you're hurting. This might be quite a challenge, but in order to forget the pain, you must be honest about what you're feeling and why. When you see it, then you can deal with it. You can pray to God honestly about it. Often we pretend we're just fine, when all we've done is buried the pain and tears. That's not being honest, and you're only hurting yourself.

Honestly, I was hurting from the relationship with my father because he didn't love me the way I needed to be loved. How long had I buried that truth in my soul? A long time.

When I was finally able to acknowledge this feeling, the Holy Spirit helped me to realize that my father had loved me the only way he could. I gave myself some slack and realized that I, too, would only be able to do my best in loving my children, and hopefully, it would be sufficient.

- Write about your feelings in a letter or journal. Writing things down helps get them out. The more you get the feelings out, the less power they have over you. You can actually *see* what you're feeling, and once you see it, you can begin to examine your feelings in depth. Writing can also help you see the progress you're making, which is encouraging.

- Remind yourself that Jesus mandates forgiveness. It's not an option, so don't think you can ignore it and be pleasing to God. Staying immersed in the scriptures and reading what Jesus said about forgetting and forgiving will keep you focused and constantly remind you why this journey is so important to your soul and spiritual life.

࿇࿇࿇

Joseph was, by all accounts, a pain in the rear. The favorite son of Jacob and Rachel, he received a lot more attention and slack than his brothers: "Now Israel loved Joseph more than any of his other sons, because he had been born to him in his old age; and he made a richly ornamented robe for him. When his brothers saw that their father loved him more than any of them, they hated him and could not speak a kind word to him." (Genesis 37:3–4)

His brothers plotted against him. At first they were going to kill him (Genesis 37:18), but then they backed off and devised another plan. They stripped him of the robe their father made for him and sold him to some Ishmaelites. The Ishmaelites took him to Egypt, where he served as a slave until he came to Pharaoh's attention:

> "The Lord was with Joseph and he prospered, and he lived in the house of his Egyptian master. When his master saw that the Lord was with him and that the Lord gave him success in everything

he did, Joseph found favor in his eyes and became his attendant."
(Genesis 39:3–4)

Joseph's value to the Egyptians increased even more when his ability to interpret dreams became known to the Pharaoh. Eventually he was put in charge of Egypt. (Genesis 41)

Joseph, then, had good fortune after being abandoned by his brothers, but no one should think that he was okay emotionally. He *Forget Not,* *Forgive Not* must have been angry with his brothers, and he may have hated them. The thought that his own flesh and blood would betray him must have eaten away at him like a lecherous parasite. He had good reason to be angry and hurt. He probably grew into his manhood with a chip on his shoulder, or at least with a chunk missing from his heart. How could he ever trust anyone again when his own flesh and blood had plotted against him? No doubt he had nightmares from time to time of being left in the pit to die. He probably imagined his brothers talking about him behind his back and congratulating themselves for getting rid of the source of their anguish. He might have told the story to several people with whom he had grown close, seeking comfort and pity for what his brothers had put him through.

Joseph was like a functioning alcoholic; in public, nobody really knew what he was feeling and how he remained drunk in his pain. Publicly, Joseph was able to forget enough of the pain to put up an effective front, find favor with God, and do what God asked.

Privately, the memory of what his brothers had done was always with Joseph. He served as king during a time when people yearned for privilege but couldn't attain it. He attained privilege despite his own brothers plotting against him. He wanted them to know that what they meant for evil, God meant for good. He wanted them to hurt like he had.

He vowed never to forget. Perhaps the vow kept him going. Perhaps he dreamed of the day he'd see his brothers again and get his revenge. He vowed that his father—still alive, though Joseph didn't know for sure—would know what had happened and would punish his brothers. He was not about to forget what had happened. The memory of it kept him going because he vowed his brothers would pay.

On another level, Joseph never expected to see his brothers

again. So, while he wanted to see them once more, if only to take his revenge, he may have written off that part of his life. He had to move forward, despite his painful past which, hopefully, was behind him.

When Pharaoh put Joseph in charge of the entire land of Egypt, I imagine Joseph felt vindicated. There he was, the boy-man who once had been left for dead but now wore a ring, fine robes of linen, and a gold chain around his neck. Once forgotten, he was elevated to a position of importance. He was driven around in a chariot, with his second-in-command shouting to the people, "Make way!"

I imagine Joseph wished his brothers could be around as Pharaoh said, "I am Pharaoh, but without your word no one will lift hand or foot in all of Egypt." (Genesis 41:44) Pharaoh gave Joseph a new name, Zaphenath-Paneah, which means "bow down," and a wife as well. Joseph was moving ahead.

Inside his soul, however, the journey was more difficult. Inside, the real coronation of grace and forgiveness hadn't yet taken place. The pain and memories that were still trapped there choked his joy, despite all the good things that were happening to him.

Joseph was thirty years old. He'd been a mere teen when his brothers had plotted to kill him. For half his life, he'd carried a toxic spirit within him. The only thing that saved him from self-destruction was the presence of the Lord in his life, giving him glimmers of hope in the midst of his spiritual wilderness.

Maybe it was that Presence that spoke to him when his sons were born. He could have named them anything. In those times, names reflected the experiences of the parents or their world at the time of the infant's birth. Joseph could have named them something that said, "For I have sought my revenge" or "Son of my misery." You know. Something that spoke to the human struggle of forgiveness that we all go through.

But during the entire time of Joseph's grieving, God was intervening in his life. Joseph somehow left enough room in his bruised spirit for the Lord to enter. Scripture says,

> "Before the years of famine, two sons were born to Joseph … Joseph named his firstborn Manasseh and said, 'It is because God has made me *forget* all my trouble and all my father's household.'

The second son he named Ephraim and said, 'It is because God has made me fruitful in the land of my suffering.'" (Genesis 41: 50–52, italics mine)

Joseph's firstborn was named Manasseh. Surely, Joseph had been praying for relief from his pain, relief from the memories of his siblings and his home, for half his young life. As he awakened day after day, he asked for deliverance from his bitterness and anger. Joseph knew that he couldn't continue to live with his spirit disintegrating within him. What had happened had happened. He couldn't change it.

So God *made him forget*. He didn't forget the incident, but he forgot the feelings that had held him captive for too long. He forgot that he needed his brothers to hurt as they'd hurt him. He forgot that too much of his time had been spent scheming and dreaming of the day when they'd hurt and he'd be able to see it. The grudge had been too consuming, too draining. God made him forget and blessed him despite all that had happened.

Joseph turned his attention from human desire to divine intervention, and he was delivered. It was that deliverance that allowed him to minister to his brothers when they later came before him. God knew that one day Joseph would come face to face with his enemies, and God wanted it to be a moment of glory for Him.

Joseph forgot, and so he could forgive. Joseph could also receive blessings from God, which God was apparently eager to give him.

Questions for Study

1. Describe a situation in which you were hurt deeply and haven't been able to let go.
2. Why are you unwilling to forget, as has been defined in this chapter?
3. What do you think you'll lose if you forget? What will you gain?
4. Has God blessed you in spite of what happened to you? Can you identify the blessings?
5. How long are you willing to hold on to your pain? Is holding onto the pain more important to you than being freed from it? Why?
6. Do you know anyone personally or in society who was hurt by

people or circumstances but was able to forget, forgive, and experience life in new and healthier ways?

7. If you disagree that forgetting is necessary or even possible write your reasons down. Share them in a group setting and discuss them.

Forgive Who?

Chapter 6
When It's Hard to Forgive Ourselves

BUT WHEN THEY HAD KINDLED A FIRE IN THE MIDDLE OF THE COURTYARD
AND HAD SAT DOWN TOGETHER, PETER SAT DOWN WITH THEM. A SERVANT
GIRL SAW HIM SEATED THERE IN THE FIRELIGHT. SHE LOOKED CLOSELY AT
HIM AND SAID, 'THIS MAN WAS WITH HIM.' BUT HE DENIED IT. 'WOMAN, I
DON'T KNOW HIM,' HE SAID."

—LUKE 22:55–57

In his book *The Sunflower*, Simon Weisenthal recalls an incident, which forever changed his life.[1] Mr. Weisenthal, a Polish Jew, was an architect in his early 20s when the Nazis overtook Germany. He watched Nazis murder his grandmother in her own home and force his mother into a railroad car filled with other Jewish women. He saw their faces and heard their screams and was distraught because he could do nothing to stop what was happening. Eighty-nine of his relatives lost their lives to the Nazis. Surely, if there was ever a person who was justified in refusing to forgive his enemies, Weisenthal was. The atrocities perpetrated against him were heinous.

Weisenthal was also put into a concentration camp and one would guess, doing all he could do to stay mentally and spiritually healthy in light of all that was going on around him. One day, he was summoned by a nurse. She asked him if he was a Jew, and when he answered in the affirmative, she asked him to follow her. Not knowing what would occur, he followed her.

She took him to a young SS soldier, who lay wounded and dying. A good part of him was bandaged, including his face where holes for his eyes, nose, and mouth had been cut out. Philip Yancey also recalls the story in his book, *What's So Amazing About Grace?* He says the encounter was a painful one. "My name is Karl," said the soldier. "I must tell you about my horrible deed, and I must tell you because you are a Jew."[2]

The soldier had been raised Roman Catholic. As a young man he'd joined the Hitler Youth Corps and later the SS. Weisenthal didn't want to hear the soldier's confession. "Three times as Karl tried to tell his story, Weisenthal pulled away as if to leave. Each time the officer reached out to grab his arm...."[3] The soldier begged Weisenthal to just listen.

The dying man recounted to Weisenthal the horror of the battle in which he had just participated. He confessed that in an act of revenge against the Russians whose booby traps had killed 30 SS soldiers, the SS had rounded up 100 Jews, "herded them into a house, doused it with gasoline and then fired grenades at it."[4] If anyone tried to escape, the young soldier rasped, they were shot.

Weisenthal didn't want to hear about the atrocity, but he listened nonetheless. Yancey says that at the end of his confession, the soldier said,

> "I am left here with my guilt. In the last hours of my life, you are with me. I do not know who you are. I know only that you are a Jew and that is enough ... I know that what I have told you is terrible. In the long nights while I have been waiting for death, time and time again I have longed to talk to a Jew and beg forgiveness from him. Only, I didn't know whether there were any Jews left. I know what I am asking is almost too much for you, but without your answer, I cannot die in peace."[5]

The young soldier was denied the peace he sought. After a few moments, Weisenthal got up and left the room without responding to the soldier's request.

I understand and sympathize with Weisenthal's decision to walk away. How dare this murderer of his family and his people even think about asking for his forgiveness!

If that had been the end of the story, I wouldn't have included it in this chapter. The fact is, however, Weisenthal was not comforted by his decision to leave the soldier without an absolution. For the rest of his life, Weisenthal was tormented by his refusal to forgive the pleading soldier. He asked many people, "What would you have done in my place?" The final section of *The Sunflower* provides some of the answers to that question.

Weisenthal's torment over not having forgiven a man who was truly repentant never left him. He couldn't forgive himself for refusing to forgive another human being.

The inability to forgive oneself is the definition of guilt. There is no greater torment than not being able to forgive oneself. Western religion has used guilt to control people by reminding us of the things we've done and how "bad" we are. We cower in churches, trying to get closer to God, but the preached word often prevents self-forgiveness from ever taking hold. If we can't forgive ourselves, grace can't do its work.

This reality didn't hit me until one day, while doing a forgiveness seminar, someone asked, "What do you do when you can't forgive yourself?" I was stymied. I hadn't thought of that dilemma. But as I thought about it, it seemed ludicrous to try to help people forgive others when they could not or would not forgive themselves.

So on the spot I asked the participants for reasons they couldn't forgive themselves. At first, they were reticent, but as more people spoke up, others followed suit:

- "I lied to my mother about stealing her bracelet to give to my girlfriend when I was 16."
- "I got caught in my parents' bed with my girlfriend when I was 16. I don't know how I could have done that!"
- "I was not a good mother for my children because when they were young, I was out in the streets, strung out on drugs."
- "I hated my father, and said I wished he would die in a fit of anger, and he died a couple of days later."
- "I gave my mother so much grief when I was a teen that I think the stress gave her cancer."
- "I cheated on my husband because I was trying to get back at him for cheating on me."
- "I didn't go through with it, but I wanted to hire someone to kill my wife. How could I think something like that?"

Quite frankly, I was surprised at the amount of personal agony and self-denigration in the room. The pain was so thick it could have been sliced through. Tears flowed freely.

I asked, "Don't you believe that God forgave you?" Some responded positively, but most avoided the question. One man then said, "Even if God forgave me, I could never forgive myself."

His response illuminated a distinctive flaw that seems to be part of the Christian walk. Christians *hear* that God forgives all, and we want to believe it, but we don't accept the veracity of that claim. The sad fact is, if we can't forgive ourselves, it's nearly impossible to forgive others.

Love operates on the same principle. If you've never experienced love, you can't give it or receive it, no matter how much someone does for you. My father once told us that he hadn't felt love when he was growing up and that it was hard for him to imagine that anyone cared for him now that he was an adult. He certainly had problems showing love to his children.

Biblically, love and forgiveness are linked. As Jesus visited the home of a Pharisee, a woman of questionable reputation "brought an alabaster jar of perfume, and as she stood behind him at his feet weeping, she began to wet his feet with her tears. Then she wiped them with her hair, kissed them and poured perfume on them." (Luke 7:37–38) The Pharisees were enraged at the woman's action.

When the woman saw Jesus, she saw a way out of her personal hell of self-hatred brought on by her past sins. She believed that Jesus accepted her, forgave her, and loved her. She knew that her peace could come only through Him. She wept as she remembered her past deeds, but she also wept for joy when Jesus forgave her and accepted her without judgment. She completely humbled herself before Him and risked being put out of the house by the disgusted and enraged Pharisees. But Jesus exonerated her even as he put the Pharisees on hold.

As this woman felt Jesus' love and forgiveness, she was able to forgive herself. If He didn't hold her past against her, neither should she. His words to the Pharisees helped: "Therefore, I tell you, her many sins have been forgiven—for she loved much. But he who has been forgiven little loves little." (Luke 7:47)

What prevents us from forgiving ourselves? Is it that we don't believe we can receive the total love of Jesus, so that we're willing to humble ourselves before Him in order to receive His grace? Or is it that we don't believe that His forgiveness could possibly include us and therefore, we're justified in not forgiving ourselves? What, then, is the basis for our being Christian? If the heart of Jesus' message is love, grace, mercy, and forgiveness, and if we refuse these gifts for ourselves, are we really following the Christ?

I can remember being in a place where I believed I was beyond God's love and forgiveness. Many of the things I'd done or even thought about doing (my mother always said either way, you were guilty) made me feel bad. I felt like I never did or said anything right. If something was wrong, I automatically assumed that my mere presence had something to do with it. I couldn't forgive myself for being me, let alone for the things I'd done in the natural course of growing up. All my life I thought I was less than everyone else.

As a child, I was adopted into a family that made me feel unworthy. They picked at me, and I picked at myself. Even when their needling stopped, mine continued. I didn't believe in myself, and I didn't believe that anyone could believe in me. I couldn't forgive myself for being different or "deficient," which was how I thought of myself. Consequently, every single negative thing that anyone said about me I accepted and internalized as being true.

I grew up believing that nothing I did was good enough for my mother. I was about ten years old when my mother told me that doctors thought my baby sister had epilepsy. I went outside on the porch and wept. My mother saw me and said sharply, "Susan! Get in here!" When I went in, she shook her finger at me and said I was wrong to cry. "How will I be able to depend on you if you cry?" Whoa! I was ashamed. I went from being scared for my baby sister to being ashamed for having human emotions and for showing them. I felt like I had let my mother down.

Much later, when I was a teen, I asked my mother to drive me to an awards ceremony. I don't remember why I hadn't invited my mother, but it wasn't because I was mad at her, or she at me. I think space was limited and we were told that if we weren't getting an award, perhaps we could ask our parents to come to the next function.

Anyway, we drove up to the location of the event, and as she was letting me out of the car my mother said, "You never invite me to any of your functions." I was floored. That wasn't true, but I couldn't understand why my mother felt that way. I automatically began to feel bad, like I was a bad person, and I didn't see how I could possibly forgive myself for hurting my mother like that, whom I dearly loved.

Then one day, when I was a young woman, I had an encounter with God. When I think of it even now I shudder because God's presence was so powerful. I was hating myself again for something, and I somehow ended up in front of the bathroom mirror. It was as though I could hear God saying to me, "Look at yourself!" I looked through tear-drenched eyes, and I heard God say, "I love you in spite of who you are, not because of who you are." I began to lay before him all of my shortcomings and misdeeds, and I could *feel* that it didn't matter to Him. It was on that day that I began to loosen the shackles of self-hatred and self-deprecation that had kept me captive for so long. ***And,*** I began to believe that God loved me. I knew that since He loved me and had forgiven me, I could forgive myself. It was only the beginning, but an important one for me.

Being able to forgive ourselves brings us in closer proximity to God. God must feel gratified that we are at least willing to try to accept the grace He's trying to give us. More than anything, I think God wants us to understand how much He loves us and how much He has invested in us. When we don't forgive ourselves, we sadden Him. He truly wants us to feel the liberation and joy of His unconditional love and acceptance. When we can do that, we can begin to accept ourselves, and use our misdeeds to help others who are having trouble believing that God's forgiveness is as complete as it is.

The starting place of our inability to forgive ourselves is usually our youth. We carry the beliefs we were taught and hold about life, as well as the opinions of people whom we first loved and respected. We learn early the concepts of "good" and "bad." In fact Western thought operates on a dichotomous paradigm. A thing is either at one end of a particular spectrum or the other; there's no middle ground. A thing is either up or down, black or white, good or bad. Western thought doesn't allow for nuances, the gray areas of consideration, as does Eastern thought. Therefore, President Bush can call Iran, Iraq, and North Korea the "axis of evil," and everyone understands and is smugly satisfied that we're not categorized as such. During the Cold War, Russia was the bad guy, which allowed the United States to be the good guy. During the McCarthy era, anyone who admitted any understanding of Communism could be labeled a Communist. Communists were bad and those who believed in Democracy were good.

In line with this kind of thinking, the mother who was caught on videotape beating her four-year old daughter was the bad guy. Some feminists would denigrate stay-at-home mothers and praise all women who work outside the home. According to pro-life advocates, women who have had abortions are bad—worse sinners than those who never had an abortion. In many churches, young women who conceive babies out of wedlock are bad and are forbidden to take part in the sacraments of the church.

We call our children bad or good, depending on how cooperative they are with adults! One of the best things I read before having my children was to resist saying "no" to them all the time, because saying no would make them feel like their natural need to grow and explore was bad. So, my children's father and I developed wonderfully creative ways to preserve their self-esteem while teaching them and protecting our house and possessions. When Charlie or Caroline would touch something that could easily be broken, we would go to them and say, "Isn't it pretty? Let's not touch it because it might fall down and not be pretty anymore." And they, with their little faces and desire to please us would understand, if only for a moment. We'd have to repeat the little dialogue many times, but what we didn't want was for them to think it was bad to be creative and inquisitive. They never broke a thing. When I look back on it, I'm still amazed. To this day they are wonderfully creative children. (In the name of creativity, I recently discovered that my son had created a mural on the wall of his bedroom. For a moment, thinking of "my white walls," I was going to be angry, but then, I smiled. I bred this sense of creativity into him. The mural remains.) I cringe when I hear parents say their babies or toddlers are bad when they cry or when they get into mischief. It creates the opportunity for demons of guilt to take hold and grow in their young spirits, making it almost impossible for them to love themselves.

Once children go to school, the bad-good paradigm kicks in full force. One is good if one learns the way the other children learn; he or she is bad if, because of higher energy levels or some other condition, he or she isn't able to sit still as long as the other children. My son, now a teen, was extremely active when he was little and was eventually put on Ritalin. He was in the second grade when he began his medication. My heart broke when, after the first day of taking it, I picked him up and he said, "Mommy, I was bad for 100 days. Now I'm a good boy."

Christianity operates on the same paradigm. We're good if we follow, not necessarily what Jesus says, but what the denomination says is the way, the truth, and the light. Some denominations say you're bad if you go to parties, put on make-up, or eat the "wrong" foods. Some denominations denounce homosexuality as the absolute worse sin of all sins. A fundamentalist group celebrated the death of Matthew Shepard, the gay man who was beaten to death. On the anniversary of his death they celebrated his "descent into hell."

All denominations have definitions of what is bad, and we must stay within our denomination's definition of good behavior if we want to get to heaven, they teach. There are at least two unfortunate drawbacks with this paradigm: 1) humans, with all of our subjective weaknesses and prejudices, become the judges of what's right and wrong, good and bad; and 2) it creates self-loathing, self deprecating Christians who can't forgive themselves.

So how should we judge right and wrong, good and bad in society? This is a difficult question because, of course, we do have to keep order in our society. Deciding right from wrong and establishing laws based on morals and values is a big part of that process. We're hampered, however, by our opinions and biases that were formed in childhood and influenced by a host of other sources and events.

Were the terrorists wrong to ram our jets into the World Trade Center and the Pentagon? Absolutely. Everyone would agree with that. The attacks were an act of murder, pure and simple.

Was it wrong for the Japanese to bomb Pearl Harbor? Most Americans would agree that it was evil and wrong. But were we right to drop the atomic bomb on Nagasaki and Hiroshima? Some would argue that we were justified; others would vehemently disagree, especially the Japanese.

Were the writers of the United States Constitution wrong to own slaves or to write that slaves were only marginally human? Are the terrorists bad? We would say yes. Were the Japanese bombers bad? Absolutely. But was Thomas Jefferson bad? Was Andrew Johnson bad for being in favor of annihilating American Indians and supporting slavery? There you'd get an argument from a lot of Americans.

The point is, humans are fairly inconsistent in determining who and what are good and bad. Some of the worse critics of homosexuality have been found to be homosexual themselves. Some of the harshest critics of drug addicts are addicted themselves or have been, and not just to chemical substances, but to gambling, sex, and other behaviors. We are poor judges of right and wrong, good and bad, and too often we overstep our bounds. We've created a society in which the people can't forgive themselves for the "wrongs" they have done.

One of the most painful moments of my ministry was when I visited a young man who was dying of AIDS. He was in the last stages of the disease, and when I visited him, he was shriveled up and lay in the fetal position, limbs hopelessly locked.

When I walked in the room, I could see terror in his eyes. It was as if he thought I was coming to condemn him. (Mind you, his sister was a deacon at a church and all of his siblings were "good" Christians.) I knew what I was seeing.

I went to his bedside and touched his arm, and he looked surprised. According to his sister, he had few visitors, and I could safely assume he was seldom touched. He recoiled when I touched him, but I told him it was alright.

I asked him to blink his eyes in answer to my questions since he was no longer able to speak: once for "yes," twice for "no." Did he know who I was? One blink. Did he feel okay today? Pause, then one blink. Was he afraid? Again, one blink. Did he think God loved him?

Tears welled up in his eyes. Very slowly, he blinked twice.

This was a gay man, on his deathbed, soon to be gone, and his spiritual agony was that God had rejected him as God's people on earth had. His sister told me he had tried to change. He had been prayed on and prayed over, but nothing seemed to help. He had wanted to be different. He just hadn't been able to change. The saints had judged and pronounced him bad, and he had accepted the verdict.

So instead of looking forward to a union and communion with a Savior who promised to forgive, accept, and receive him, this man was dying with the additional burden of not being able to forgive himself.

Forgive Who?

When I left his room, I wept.

ададада

If we take the time, we can think of lots of reasons why it's hard to forgive ourselves. Some of us are more capable than others of letting go of self-hatred, but many of us struggle with accepting our weaknesses and mistakes our whole lives. We absorb our mistakes like a good towel absorbs moisture and are robbed of the freedom of feeling God's forgiveness. More importantly, we project the discontent in our spirits onto others who have their own weaknesses to deal with. What we see in them, we've not been able to forgive in ourselves. And if someone accuses us of something that's true and for which we haven't forgiven ourselves, we feel condemned and unworthy of forgiveness.

If someone says something about us that we know isn't true, and we haven't forgiven ourselves, we are unable to stand strong against the accusation. There's a nagging sense of "what if?" that haunts us, making us absorb a guilt that is not ours. Once we've learned to forgive ourselves, however, we're able to place the issue in God's court, so to speak, and are reassured that He loves us, regardless of our shortcomings. It's a blessed state of liberation!

If sin can be defined as "anything that separates us from God," then not forgiving ourselves is one of the biggest sins going. Contrary to what many of us have been taught, sin is not as simple as being good or bad. It's much deeper than that. Sin negatively affects our ability to be in a loving relationship with God. When we don't practice self-forgiveness, we separate ourselves from God's peace and presence. Self-loathing is one of the most debilitating of sins.

Unfortunately, too many of us have too many reasons for not liking ourselves. Being told, for example, that our hair is too thick or our lips are too big can make us loath those parts of our bodies until we die. Being told by a parent that we're stupid or unable to achieve, that it's our fault that the family is messed up, can do irreparable damage. We carry those messages for a long time.

When It's Hard to Forgive Ourselves

But we forget that "all have sinned and fall short of the glory of God." (Romans 3:23) We beat ourselves up instead of giving ourselves some slack and giving the guilt to God. When we give the guilt to God, we begin to experience the power of forgiveness. Giving God our guilt, also known as repenting, is absolutely necessary for self-forgiveness to "take."

There's a difference between being sorry and being repentant. We can say we're sorry and not mean it—or mean it and engage in the same behavior again and again. When I was little, we weren't allowed to fight, so when we did, we'd get in trouble. My mother would make us, on pain of being punished, say we were sorry. We'd apologize only because she was standing there threatening us.

We really weren't sorry. Often, late at night after she'd fallen asleep, we'd pick up the fight where we'd left off. Anyone can say he or she is sorry. Saying you're sorry buys you time and maybe some sympathy or lenience. People who engage in domestic violence or even driving while drunk are constantly saying they're sorry, but their behavior says that what they're sorry about is having been caught.

When you're repentant, however, you desire to change. The memory of what you've done grieves you so much that you'll do anything not to repeat the behavior again. Being repentant is the first step toward being able to feel God's forgiveness and thus being able to forgive oneself.

When we're repentant, there's no need to carry guilt about things we've done (or not done), whether long ago or recently. True repentance opens the door to God's power, and our lives begin to change. The reasons you've hated yourself begin to pale in comparison to God's love for and forgiveness of you. For example:

- You stole your best friend's boyfriend or girlfriend.
- You cheated on your spouse.
- You stole money from your family to support your gambling or drug habit.
- You lied to your best friend and double-crossed her in order to get a job.

- You were supposed to be watching your baby sibling but took your eyes away for a moment, and she/he drowned.
- You knew you were pregnant and should have stopped smoking and doing drugs, but you didn't, and your baby was born with congenital defects.
- You didn't tell the one person you loved most that you had a sexually transmitted disease and passed it on. He/she died.
- You never told your mother you loved her.
- You always argued with your parents and gave them a hard time.
- You weren't there for your children when they were young. Now, one doesn't talk to you, another treats you with polite respect but no warmth, and another is in jail.
- Your lie on the witness stand resulted in an innocent person going to prison.

Repentance allows us to know it's not necessary for us to beat ourselves up forever for our transgressions. Once we stop beating ourselves, we can stop beating others. Until we stop the self-flagellation, we're enslaved to a past that we cannot change. Subconsciously, we think we're not sorry enough if we're able to forgive ourselves. We think that in order to make a good impression on God, we have to continually show Him our remorse. It's the same kind of thinking that says we must look and feel sad forever when a loved one dies. To be free of grief too quickly is to somehow desecrate the memory of our loved one. We think love means *showing* sadness to people, and that's just not true. We are obligated to reveal a repentant spirit to God. That's love.

Some people think they're being religious when they're hard on themselves and others. The fact is that our inability to forgive ourselves prevents us from being able to help others. Our mistakes are not our crosses; they are our crowns. When we forgive ourselves as God has forgiven us, we're then free to minister to others who think they'll never be worthy of being close to God because of the mistakes they've made. God wants to use "unworthy," sick people to reach others who are sick. He wants to use people who've "been there," have gotten out, and who can help others navigate the course.

How many of us are carrying guilt that's eating us alive and making us miserable because we can't forgive ourselves? Deep down, we don't believe God or any human can forgive us either. When we don't forgive ourselves, we block God's power and mercy in our lives. When we take that first self-forgiving step, however, God's power and mercy will begin to liberate us from self-loathing, humiliation, and shame. We get to the point where we *have* to forgive ourselves and others because God's forgiveness of us is so incredible, so awesome, so *healing*.

When It's Hard to Forgive Ourselves

It doesn't matter how much you messed up. Forgiving yourself is a must. Ask Peter.

⋄⋄⋄⋄⋄

Peter was one of the original Twelve, chosen by Jesus personally. He was never a choirboy. Personality studies of the disciples show that Peter was impetuous, impulsive, quick-tempered, and impatient. He probably hurt a lot of people in his day, not because he was bad, but because he was brusque and arrogant. He would say and do things that wouldn't go over well with his peers or even with his superiors.

By the time Jesus called Peter, a fisherman by trade, to be a disciple, he was probably aware of his shortcomings. In spite of himself, Peter felt honored to have been called. But I imagine he may have balked, and wondering why Jesus would call the likes of him. We don't know what Peter struggled with, but we can safely assume that he carried some memories of events from his past that he was ashamed of and for which he had not forgiven himself and had therefore deemed himself unworthy to walk with Jesus.

Later, as Peter learned about forgiveness from the Master, maybe he began to work through offenses he'd committed in the past. Maybe he began to realize that Jesus accepted him just as he was, and that enabled Peter to forgive himself and become an effective disciple.

But alas, forgiveness notwithstanding, our weaknesses remain with us. They're our agents of humility. They remind us that no matter how far we've come, we're never really far from where we were. They let us know that in order to stay the course we *need* God. Peter may not have realized this fact, but Jesus did.

That's why he told an incredulous Peter shortly before He was to die that he, Peter, would deny even knowing him. At that moment, Peter must have cringed and realized that Jesus knew him better than he thought. Peter had had a hard time fitting into the Twelve. He liked being part of mainstream society, and he liked being liked. Jesus' teachings had often resulted in the Twelve being shunned and ostracized. Although Peter never jumped ship, he was always bothered by the rejections. He didn't like being talked about or set apart. Oh, he realized it was an honor to have been chosen by this man Jesus, but there was a part of his personality that just wanted to be free and enjoy life more. He wanted to associate with whomever he wanted, as well as being one of Jesus' own. When he couldn't have his cake and eat it too, it bothered him.

Following Jesus was a risky and often deadly life, and Peter wanted to live. He wasn't ready to die, nor did he want to suffer as many of the Twelve already had. He wasn't willing to die for Jesus, though his passion might belie that fact. He wasn't willing to be tortured on behalf of Jesus, and the possibility of torture was very real. Because of his personality, desires, wishes, and ambition, there were limits to his discipleship.

Jesus knew it and looked sadly when Peter tried to reassure Him. "Even if all fall away on account of you, I never will," said Peter.

"This man does not know himself," Jesus must have thought. "He does not know what my Father has already seen and forgiven and what Peter will have to see and forgive in himself."

And so Jesus answered him, "I tell you the truth ... this very night, before the rooster crows, you will disown me three times.' (Matthew 26:34) Peter was aghast. How could Jesus think such a thing? Maybe he would disown someone else, but not Jesus. Yes, he wanted to fit into his village, into his society, but not at the cost of disowning Jesus. Surely, Jesus knew that!

But Jesus didn't alter his statement. When Peter protested, saying, "Even if I have to die with you, I will never disown you," Jesus must have smiled. (Matthew 26:35)

Peter, Jesus, and the others went to Gethsemane. A few hours passed, and Peter witnessed the horror of Jesus' betrayal by Judas. He watched as angry soldiers, apparently not interested in truth but only in their assignment to remove Jesus from the scene, intruded on the quiet of Gethsemane. He listened as people outside the walls of Gethsemane, who had only a week before hailed Jesus as King of the Jews, now railed against him and called for his death. To Peter, it was amazing, unbelievable and frightening. Jesus had predicted his death, sure, but never in Peter's wildest imagination did he imagine it would be like this. People weren't *listening*. Any fool would have been able to see that something was wrong. Peter realized that he never really believed that Jesus would die.

He'd been wrong, and now he was scared. Jesus *was* going to die, or at least suffer a great deal, and Peter didn't want to experience the same thing.

After Jesus had been seized, in an act of love, terror, and fear Peter cut off a soldier's ear, only to have Jesus heal it immediately. The disciple was emotionally worn out. A part of him probably wondered why Jesus hadn't told the disciples that it would be like *this*. Maybe they could have prepared, done something, anything. But it was useless to think that way. Peter followed Jesus as the soldiers pushed Him and beat Him, taking Him to some trial that Peter knew would not be fair. And Jesus wasn't even fighting back.

They reached the courtyard, Jesus, the soldiers, and the crowd, and kindled a fire. Peter was exhausted and scared. Surely, if they treated Jesus this badly, and he was blameless, what would they do to *him* who could not even come close to claiming the same?

As he wrestled with his thoughts and fears, a servant girl looked at his face, which glowed in the fire. Peter turned away to avoid making contact. When he looked up again, she was still staring, and then she said it: "This man was with him."

"Oh goodness," he thought, desperately. "Please don't point me out." This was Peter, desperate now to be safe and unscathed by human evil and unfair treatment. This was Peter, the man with ambitions, his relationship with Jesus notwithstanding. Going through a trial because of his relationship with Jesus was not part of the plan. He didn't want to suffer any more than he had, just being a disciple. He wasn't as strong as Jesus. He could never hold up.

"Woman, I don't know him." Peter heard himself saying the awful words. How could he do that? Jesus had been nothing but good to him. Had taken him in and nurtured him. How could he do this?

Yet, the part of him that Jesus knew well was in full regalia. Much as he wanted to shake it, he couldn't. A man recognized him as being one of the Twelve. Perhaps this man remembered some lesson that Peter had given while walking with the Master.

"Man, I am not!" Peter replied with some energy. His voice was sharp, threatening.

At that point, Peter should have been able to draw on something that Jesus had taught him to keep his "thorn" under control, but he couldn't, didn't, or both. An hour later, another person said, "Certainly, this fellow was with him, for he is a Galilean."

Peter, now desperately afraid, said angrily, "Man, I don't know what you're talking about!"

The cock crowed.

It was a horrible moment. Mind you, Jesus was not far from Peter and the crowd when this was all going on. He never even acknowledged that he heard the conversations or his disciple. But when the cock crowed, "The Lord turned and looked straight at Peter." (Luke 26:61)

Peter remembered Jesus' prediction. He went away and wept bitterly.

Does anyone *not* think Peter had a hard time forgiving himself? Not only did he deny knowing Jesus, but Jesus, in the throes of suffering, had actually heard him do it. Peter didn't have the luxury of denying in secret the One who counted most. His sin, his weakness, his thorn, lay before him, fully exposed.

What next? Curl up from guilt, or ask Jesus to forgive him and help him forgive himself?

Peter must have chosen the second option. Maybe Jesus gave

him a gentle prod, telling him that he was forgiven and that he, Peter, should use this experience to minister to others, to tell others that there was NO sin that Jesus wouldn't forgive.

I imagine Jesus told Peter, "The only way to move forward is to forgive yourself and accept My forgiveness of you. Hold your head up. Tell what you did and how I freed you. Tell how forgiving yourself gave you the freedom to talk about your transgression, and use this example to help someone else.

When It's Hard to Forgive Ourselves

"More importantly, talk about how forgiving yourself loosed that yoke from around your neck and made you rejoice at being given a second chance."

I have to believe that Peter, while never forgetting what he did, forgave himself and was, therefore, able to throw guilt off his spirit and into the sea. It didn't happen immediately, but I imagine it did happen.

Forgiving ourselves is necessary to exorcise the demons that rejoice when we beat ourselves into a guilt-induced malaise.

Jesus wouldn't have it any other way.

❧❧❧❧

Simon Weisenthal, the Jew who couldn't forgive himself because he didn't forgive the dying SS soldier, shows us how lack of self-forgiveness can stymie our spiritual growth. If we don't forgive ourselves, we're doomed to perpetual torment that cannot be assuaged by revenge, money, or anything the world has to offer.

Being able to forgive oneself opens the door to feeling God's love, which can heal any hurt. Philip Yancey asks, "Which carries the higher cost, forgiveness or unforgiveness?"[6]

Questions for Study

1. Do you need to forgive yourself for something you did in the past? Write the incident(s) down as you remember them.
2. Why haven't you forgiven yourself? Can you forgive yourself? Do you think your transgression is beyond the scope of God's mercy?

3. How is your behavior toward others affected by your lack of self-forgiveness?
4. What do you have to do first to begin forgiving yourself? Do you have to see the person? Clear up confusion around the situation or event?
5. What do you stand to lose by forgiving yourself? What will you gain?

6. Has the person you offended forgiven you? Even if the person has not forgiven you, can you forgive yourself or is your self-forgiveness contingent upon him/her forgiving you? Why? Where is God in all of this?
7. Do you believe God has forgiven you?
8. Do you believe you're worthy of God's forgiveness?
9. What was the lesson you learned from your transgression?
10. What would you have done if you'd been in Simon Weisenthal's shoes? Could you have forgiven the soldier? Did Weisenthal's inability to forgive the dying soldier contribute to his own life-long torment? Why or why not?

Chapter 7
When It's God's Fault

My God, my God, why have you forsaken me? Why are you so far off from saving me?"
—Psalm 22:1

The room was dark and silent except for the labored breathing of the young man lying on the bed. He was dying and everyone knew it. He was so young. He had two young children, too young to be left without a father. He was a man who loved his community and was always trying to help someone. A role model. That's what he was.

When he was diagnosed with multiple myeloma, he paused. Well, this will be a fight," he said, "but I'll win because I have God on my side." His enthusiasm inspired all who loved him and certainly fed their faith.

He got through chemotherapy with flying colors. It was gratifying and a testimony to his faith in God. It was going to be another Lance Armstrong kind of miracle—everyone believed it.

But after three months of the cancer being in remission, the faithful disciple knew something was wrong. He felt so bad, and he knew in his heart the dreaded disease was making a comeback. After some delay he visited his doctor, who confirmed his worst fears. Not only had it come back, but it was spreading at an alarming speed. The doctors could do nothing more for him.

As he now lay in his room, dying, his wife stared straight ahead. Her eyes were blank; she said little. Her husband struggled to stay alive, and she stroked his hand lightly, telling him to hold on. When he finally took his last breath, she bent over and kissed him and walked out of the room.

Tears streaming down her face she said bitterly, "I will *never* forgive God for taking him. Never." Everyone knew to leave her alone.

રાજરા

Sometimes it's God's fault.

Well, not really. But that's what we think. God is supposed to be kind, loving, good, just, and *preferential to those who call Him their own.* We believe that God is supposed to honor us for believing in Him, and that means making sure bad things don't happen to us.

One of the resounding questions that was asked after September 11, 2001, was "Why didn't God prevent it?" Nobody came up with an answer. It's safe to say that many people blame God for the pain they've suffered since that awful day.

As believers, we often get into trouble when we think that God is supposed to do our will as opposed to the other way around. When God doesn't do what we want, we have spiritual temper tantrums. We wrestle with the bad things that come our way, and we conclude that our pain and suffering is God's fault.

I blamed God for my mother's death. She had ovarian cancer, which metastasized. It began as a cyst on her ovary. The doctor decided that the cyst was harmless, a female thing. Less than six months later she had her annual chest x-ray and white stuff was found all over her lungs. They thought she had tuberculosis, then sarcoidosis. Wrong on both counts. After being in the hospital for four months, suffering excruciating headaches, not being able to hold food down, and taking more tests than a human body should, they concluded that she had ovarian cancer. By the time they figured it out, it had spread everywhere.

That was in April. She died a month later, and I blamed God.

I blamed Him because I didn't believe He had acted as God should have. He could have whispered to the first doctor that the "cyst" was something more. Better yet, He could have wiped out all traces of the cancer at the outset. He is God, after all, the One who created the heavens and the universe, the One who somehow figured out how to make the stars form figures in the sky. He's the One who figured out how to configure human cells so they'd form a perfect human body, complete with a brain that can figure out the most amazing things. So wiping cancer from my beloved mother ought not to have been a problem.

I blamed Him because I believed He'd been unfair and that He could have prevented it. Honestly, I asked Him why He hadn't taken my stepfather instead. I wasn't close to him. He'd adopted me to make me "his own," but I never felt like his. But my mom … *ah!* She was my heart, and God knew it! Why in the *world* would He have dishonored my spirit like that? He knew how her death would affect me. He could have prevented it all.

Oh yes, I was mad at God, and it took a long time for me to get over it. It took me a long time to forgive Him for taking her. It was His fault, I believed, and my anger at Him festered for years.

Many wrestle with why bad things happen to good people. We know it, but we don't think it's fair or right. We are God's people, for goodness sake. He's supposed to be our Divine Parent, and parents strive to get the best for their children.

We can't prevent bad things from happening to our own children. Our children get killed playing sports, driving cars, hanging out with friends. Try as hard as we might to protect and control them, we can't do it, and they wouldn't let us if we tried anyway. We can't prevent them from falling down or hanging out with people who are horrible influences. We can't prevent our daughters from marrying abusive men or our sons from connecting with manipulative women. We can't go to school with them and watch their every move, *nor do we want to.* Part of being a parent is letting go and letting them find out who they are and what they can or can't take. When we let them go, when they're no longer under our constant protection, some bad things are bound to happen.

Immature children usually blame their parents for their bad luck. "If my mother had loved me more, I wouldn't be on drugs." "If my father had been home, I wouldn't be in prison." We find comfort in blaming our parents, *our saviors,* because it's easier to do that than face our own issues. Though we fight them for our independence, we really think they're supposed to do our bidding and save us when our bad decisions cause us some pain or discomfort.

It doesn't work that way on earth, and apparently, it doesn't work that way in heaven either.

My son recently entered high school and made the freshman soccer team. He'd been asking for contact lenses for a while and I was getting around to it. Money was a little tight and he had to wait because he had to get an eye exam in order to get the lenses. He insisted that he had to have them to play soccer, and I wearily listened and acknowledged that I had heard the need.

Well, one day he came home mad. "Mom," he screamed, "I *told* you I needed lenses!" He'd gotten hit in the face with the soccer ball and his poor little glasses were all bent up. He was livid, not at the ball, the player, or the coach, but at *me* for not moving quickly enough to meet his needs. Now his glasses were messed up and it was my fault.

The incident showed me how we relate to God. He *wearily listens while we spew our desires at Him.* My son truly needed the lenses, but many times, he spews out a "need" when it's really something he wants. In the meantime I asked him, "What have you done lately for someone else? Why are you always asking for stuff that you really don't need? Why do you get mad when you don't get your way?"

I think this is how God regards us sometimes, because if the truth be told, the only time many of us pray is when we want something. It wearies God. Then, when we don't get what we need, when our glasses get all bent up because life has hit us in the face, we get mad at God. Like spoiled children, we don't forgive Him for a long time.

Some might buy that argument; others would not, and justifiably so. Some would say that they don't just pray when they want something; they pray constantly, not asking for things but thanking God for being in their lives. They have an honest to goodness relationship with Him. Surely that counts for something. So when bad things happen to people who fall into this category, their pain is even greater. In this instance, the unfortunate occurrence in their lives feels like an honest betrayal, and it's hard to swallow.

When we think about our unwillingness to forgive God, often it doesn't seem that the anger was rational. One of my members shared why she'd been unable to forgive God. "My foster father was the only person in the whole world who knew who my real mother and family were," she said. "He died before he could let me know who she was and I felt like God allowed him to die with my secret. I was angry for a very long time, and God knew it."

This woman couldn't understand why God had treated her so badly. She was a regular churchgoer, a tither, a good mother, a woman who had made a conscious effort to live as God wanted her to. All she wanted, she said, was to know who her real mother was. She had suffered a lot not knowing, especially growing up in a house where her siblings constantly reminded her that she was not "one of them." "For a long time, that's all I asked for," she said. "My foster father always said he'd let me know when I was old enough. But he died when I was young, and nobody else knew who she was."

Her pain, she concluded, was God's fault, and even if she had wanted to forgive Him, she couldn't. She felt like He had reneged on his duties, and she just couldn't understand.

❧❧❧

As an African American, I was mad at God for the longest time because I felt He allowed black people to suffer at the hands of white people who were filled with hatred. I didn't get it. God could change hearts. Surely, as a loving parent He didn't *want* us to suffer! Why was He allowing bad people to advance in life while they trampled over innocent people who genuinely believed in Him and always gave Him his due? How could He just stand by and let discrimination exist that tore out the hearts and spirits of so many of the faithful? Where was He when people were being lynched and tortured just for being black? Where was He when those little children, trying to integrate a school in Little Rock, Arkansas, were being taunted by all those white people?

It seemed to me that God had disregarded some of His people while telling us to "forgive" our enemies. I thought His expectations were crazy and unfair. When it became apparent that forgiveness of the enemy was necessary to get to heaven, I for one turned the anger inside and had a hard time forgiving God for even requiring such a thing. I also had a hard time forgiving God for allowing black people to be the "scourge of the earth." Surely He knew what people of African descent—actually, what anyone who was not white—would suffer. So why had He even created the different races?

As I got older, my anger at God increased when I realized that racists used the Bible as justification for their actions. I got angry when I watched white people worship. They seemed so genuine, yet I

89

couldn't conceive that the God they worshipped was the same one I worshipped. Their God condoned racism and discrimination. Their God allowed churches to exclude people on the basis of race. Philip Yancey said that the deacons at his church (openly racist) had a card they gave to black people who came to worship with them that read,

Forgive Who?

"Believing the motives of your group to be ulterior and foreign to the teaching of God's word, we cannot extend a welcome to you and respectfully request you to leave the premises quietly. Scripture does NOT teach 'the brotherhood of man and the fatherhood of God.' He is the Creator of all, but only the Father of those who have been regenerated. If any one of you is here with a sincere desire to know Jesus Christ as Savior and Lord, we shall be glad to deal individually with you from the Word of God."[1]

Yancey identifies this as a "unanimous statement of pastor and deacons, August, 1960."[2]

I didn't know about statements like that when I was young, but I could see the images on television and knew that Martin Luther King wrote a letter to Christian ministers from a Birmingham jail. I knew white people kept black people out of their churches, wouldn't let them drink water from the same fountains nor swim in the same pools. It made me mad, but my mother said it was necessary to forgive white people. What she didn't know was that forgiving white people was only part of my requirement. I was struggling to forgive *God* for disliking black people and making whites so evil.

A Jewish friend of mine expressed some of the same sentiments regarding God and His apparent nonintervention in the Holocaust.

"For the longest time, I couldn't really pray. My parents did, and my grandparents did, but I couldn't. I asked my mother one time how she could forgive God. It was His fault! He had created Hitler and He had allowed Hitler to kill off his 'chosen people.' I asked her how she could forgive God, and my mother said she couldn't, really. She just had to forget and move on."

Forget? My friend couldn't forget, and so forgiveness was im possible. She said she'd worship God, but with a chip on her shoulder. A disappointing God was better than no God at all, but just barely, she said. She didn't have a lot of faith that He would really take care of His children.

Another friend shared with me that she hadn't forgiven God because of her parents. Her mother had an affair with a married man and she, my friend, was one of the results of that indiscretion. Her mother deserted her, and she never knew her father.

> "As a child growing up in church, I was taught that God loves and protects his children," she said. "I was taught that the things that happened were God's will. God is the one who gives us our parents. We were taught that he had our lives planned for us even before we were born. So why would He *plan* for some of us to suffer?"

As a child, she'd been sexually and physically abused, all the while going to church and hearing how good God was. It didn't mesh. Her mother made the decision to give her away. And God was good?

She said, "I questioned why the Lord didn't protect me from the sexual abuse I received as a child. He saw it. He knew it was going on. Why didn't He protect me?"

She concluded that she was unworthy of God's love. "Had I been better, I would have gotten better," she said. "I just knew I didn't deserve to be loved. But I never forgave God because His desertion of me implied that I wasn't worthy of His time and attention."

ᏗᏗᏗᏗ

We confront at least two problems as we wrestle with our relationship with God. One is that we're held captive by an Old Testament notion of how the Lord works. That notion is that God gives good things to good people and makes bad things happen to bad people. The second problem is that we believe that if we're good people we're not supposed to suffer. If we do, it means that God deems us unworthy of protection or favor.

Maybe we should back into this discussion by mentioning that according to the Christian Bible, God allowed two people to suffer, Job and Jesus. He didn't cause their pain; He just didn't prevent it from happening. He didn't protect Him from an unjust situation. He did it not because He didn't love Jesus, but because He loved US so much that he used his only Son to save us.

It may not make sense, but that's the honest truth.

If it's supposed to make us feel better to hear that God doesn't cause suffering, it doesn't. We don't feel comforted knowing that He allows us to hurt sometimes. Many of us wrestle with the story of Job, where God makes a wager with Satan using Job as the pawn. God didn't cause Job's horrible sequence of events. He allowed Satan to tempt Job as long as Satan didn't "lay a finger" on him. Big deal.

But the power of the story of Job is that it allows us to see how God has worked through history. God knew about the Holocaust and allowed it. He knew what African Americans would suffer just for having dark skin and allowed it. He knew that my friend would suffer as a child but allowed it. And through it all, we learn in hindsight, God was "there" all the time. It is little comfort to us while we are going through the fire.

When things like this happen, we doubt God on three levels: we doubt His omniscience, omnipotence, and omnipresence. Surely, if God knew all things, had power over all things, and was everywhere at all times, the vast amount of the suffering His children endure would be prevented.

Our doubts show that we don't understand God as a parent who knows what He is doing. So what should we believe? That God doesn't care—about the Holocaust, African American slavery, or any other atrocity? That's even more distasteful. What's left is anger at God because we really don't understand Him, how He works, or why He allows bad things to happen to us.

Secondly, God didn't make a bad thing happen to a bad person. In the story of Job, we know that God allowed a bad thing to happen to a good person, but stayed in the mix. He wasn't far off. He was rather like a parent who knowingly allows something "bad" to happen to his or her child because a point has to be made. The parent is right there, ready to rescue the child when it is time.

I've done that with my own children. When my son was about four years old, I picked him up from daycare every day. It would get late, and as a busy mom with lots more to do in the waning hours of the day, I was always in a rush to get home.

One day during the Christmas season, I went to pick up my son as usual. In the lobby of the daycare were lots of gifts that could be purchased. When I went to get my son, for some reason, he didn't want to leave. He protested when I picked him up. So I put him down. He was an energetic child, but on this day, he made it his business to walk very slowly.

"Hurry up, Charlie," I said. "We've got to go." But he was in no mood to cooperate. When he got to the lobby, he languished at the little tables filled with magical trinkets, coat still dragging behind him.

"Hurry up, Charlie," I repeated as patiently as I could. He ignored me. Now I was getting mad, but I had to find a creative way to get him to do my will and not his.

"Charlie, if you don't hurry up, I'll have to leave you here." No response.

My daughter was also with me. Frustrated, I took her outside, pretending to leave. I looked behind me; Charlie had not budged. I got into the car and looked toward the front door. No Charlie. I pulled up in the driveway so that Charlie could see that we were in the car, ready to go.

He didn't move.

So I pulled away slowly, thinking he'd come speeding out of the school, repentant and lovable again. It didn't happen. I had no choice. *Though I knew it was risky and that he would be terrified,* I pulled out of the parking lot and headed to a convenience store up the hill. When I got to the store, I went inside and called the school. I could hear Charlie screaming in the background. *"Mommy! Mommy!"*

Of course, the sound of his pain and the knowledge of his fear drove a stake into my heart. I scurried back down the hill and picked up my son, who was very angry that I had left him to suffer, but glad I was *right there.*

That's how God works. He will allow us to suffer, sometimes

for our own good and sometimes because of reasons only He knows. *But He is always there.*

How does this idea play out in light of the Holocaust, American slavery, or September 11, 2001? What about God's omnipotence? Where does His power play into the equation? Why didn't it manifest itself *like we needed it to?* Who cares about His presence, His "always being there," if we suffer anyway? Is God for us or against us? We don't believe God was there, or if He was, He shirked on His duties.

God doesn't seem to understand, we reason, that we need Red Sea experiences in the here and now. He saved the Israelites by parting the Red Sea just long enough for them to get to the other side. Why doesn't God make Himself known like that in our day and age?

These questions nag at our very spiritual cores. Those who've lived through calamities can testify that God was responsible for their survival and that He was near. How many 9-11 stories were told of people calling on God as they crawled through fire and smoke and death? How many of our slave ancestors called on God during lynchings, beatings, rapes, and injustice, and derived strength from His presence? How many Jewish people acknowledge that even in concentration camps, they called on God to deliver them? All of these suffering servants somehow knew that God was near, and they knew that if they were to survive, it would be because of God.

It's those who cannot acknowledge God's nearness who have the hardest time forgiving Him for their pain.

There's a bigger problem. We really are Old Testament believers in a lot of ways. In addition to believing that we are biblically mandated to give "an eye for an eye and a tooth for a tooth," we honestly believe that bad things are supposed to happen to bad people and good things to good people. So when good people suffer and hurt, our belief system can't provide us reasons why.

In the Gospel of John, upon seeing a blind man, Jesus' own disciples asked Him, "Rabbi, who sinned, this man or his parents, that he was born blind?" (John 9:1)

The disciples' question was valid, based on the understanding and teaching of scripture. In giving the Ten Commandments, the Lord Himself said, "For I, the Lord your God, am a jealous God punishing the children for the sin of the father to the third and fourth generation of those who hate me." (Exodus 20:5B) Again, in the Book of Exodus, Moses proclaims that "He does not leave the guilty unpunished; he punishes the children and their children for the sin of the fathers to the third and fourth generation." (Exodus 34:7)

Watching Job suffer his friend Eliphaz says, "Consider now: Who, being innocent, has ever perished? Where were the upright ever destroyed?" (Job 4:7) Eliphaz concludes that the unjust were destroyed "by the breath of God." (Job 4:9A) Even one of the most glorious Psalms of the Bible, Psalm 37, communicates this opinion: "I was young and now I am old, yet I have never seen the righteous forsaken or their children begging for bread." (Psalm 37:25)

Those beliefs, unfortunately, have been taught boldly and repeatedly, too often at the exclusion of other biblical texts, which are seemingly contradictory. Jehoash, son of Jehoahaz, a king of Israel,

> "executed the officials who had murdered his father the king. Yet he did not put the sons of the assassins to death, in accordance with what is written in the Book of the Law of Moses where the Lord commanded: 'Fathers shall both be put to death for their children, nor children put to death for their fathers; *each person is to die for his own sins.*'" (2 Kings 14:5–6, italics mine)

In the Book of Ezekiel, it is written: "the soul who sins is the one who will die." (Ezekiel 18:4) More explicitly, the prophet writes that the righteous "will not die for his father's sin; he will surely live. But his father will die for his own sin...." (Exodus 18:17–18)

Those passages help give a different perspective on the too common belief that people suffer because of something someone else did. They are proof that the Bible is at best contradictory when it comes to the question of who suffers and why. But they still don't clear up the belief that bad things happen to bad people and good things to good people at the direction of God.

The only way past that idea is through Jesus. He was a good person, perfect, actually, yet something bad and unjust happened to Him. As Christians, we might expect to suffer some, in our own ways, as did He, but if we grasp the reality of His experience, we understand that sometimes good people suffer.

That being the case and the truth, how do we forgive God for it?

How do we forgive God for being made to feel unworthy of His love or attention by well-meaning preachers (some of them)? How do we forgive God for allowing circumstances in our lives that ripped us apart? How do we forgive Him for allowing our children to die too early or our parents to be killed in some freak accident? How do the parents of Laci Peterson forgive Him for allowing their pregnant daughter to be brutally murdered? Has John Walsh been able to forgive God for not preventing the kidnapping and murder of his son Adam?

How do people who have been wrongfully imprisoned for crimes they truly did not commit forgive God? How do the faithful, praying parents forgive God for not making sure a heart became available for their child before it was too late? Surely, God being God could have made things different to our liking.

The answer isn't easy. It actually takes a fair amount of spiritual maturity to forgive God *in spite of the pain in our lives.* It also takes a fair amount of time. I know a woman who loved God but who was bitterly angry within Him after her husband died unexpectedly of a heart attack. For years, she would not step foot into her church or any church. When I finally saw her again, at least 10 years later, I was surprised; it was in church. "I had to stay away from church and from God, Rev. Sue," she said. "I couldn't forgive Him for taking the only man I've ever loved." This woman doubted God's compassion when He took her husband knowing how important he'd been to her. He had been her first and only love. She couldn't understand. As I listened to her talk, I could relate because I wondered the same things when my mother died. Throughout my life I've wondered about God's love and compassion when He allowed some of His own people to suffer so mercilessly. It didn't seem right. It never seems right.

While we are in the muck of our pain, the best we can do is trust in the foundation we've already built. That foundation will subconsciously acknowledge His nearness, even if we cannot verbalze it. The experience is rather like us being angry with our parents. Though we're hurt and we distance ourselves from them, in the back of our minds we know they're near. We remember the love they've shown us in the past and the love we've shown them. During difficult times, we take the memory of their love "to the bank" and cash in on it. Whether we acknowledge it or not, it preserves us.

So, we survive by remembering God's love and presence in our lives before we started hurting. We survive by remembering that He never promised us that we would never suffer and always have things just as we want. He did promise that He would never leave us alone. His nearness gives us comfort and the strength to get through the suffering. Always, His nearness gives us doses of divine inspiration and hope at our times of greatest need.

"Do not let your hearts be troubled. Trust in God; trust also in me … I will not leave you as orphans; I will come to you." (John 14:1, 18)

Questions for Study

1. Write about a time when you had trouble forgiving God. What happened?

2. How do you think God is supposed to act? Compare that to how He really acts?

3. Why do you think God allows bad things to happen to good people? Is there any advantage in His letting those things happen?

4. Do you derive any comfort from reading that you are not suffering because of something your parents did? Did you grow up believing that you were somehow cursed to suffer because of your family history?

5. How does the concept of the "nearness of God" assuage your spirit when thinking of how you've suffered?

6. If God allows suffering to happen, does that, in your opinion, mean that He is less omnipotent?

7. Do you need a God who prevents bad things from happening to you in order to more fully believe in Him?

8. If you do not feel the nearness of God personally, is there something you can do to change that aspect of your relationship with Him? Do you want to?

Chapter 8
Acknowledging Your Part

"When he came to his senses, he said, 'How many of my father's hired men have food to spare, and here I am starving to death! I will set out and go back to my father and say to him: Father, I have sinned against heaven and against you.'"

—Luke 15:17–18

The young woman sat in my office in tears. Her marriage was on the rocks and she was tired of trying to make things work. The marriage had been difficult from the beginning.

A note of self-righteousness kept creeping up in her comments. She clearly blamed her husband for their marital problems and absolved herself of all responsibility. After she'd gotten it all out, I asked her, "What was your part in all of this?"

She looked at me incredulously and then angrily. "How could you ask that?" she hissed. "You heard my story. I didn't play around. I stayed at home, took care of his children, washed his clothes, and cooked his food. I was there. I didn't break the vows. He did. I did *nothing* wrong."

The upset wife, angry with me for suggesting she had anything to do with her dilemma, chose to absolve herself of any blame. Her husband was the bad one, not her. I told her that no situation is ever one-sided. Whether inadvertently or on purpose, we contribute to situations in ways that aren't in our best interest.

"From what you tell me, this marriage is about over," I said to her. "But there is more at stake here. If you're going to heal and get on with your life, you're going to have to forgive him and forgive yourself."

She tensed. "Forgive myself for *what?*" she asked sharply.

"Forgive yourself for whatever you did, even unknowingly, that may have contributed to what happened. For example, you could start by forgiving yourself for marrying him." She was quiet, and I took advantage of the opportunity.

"Whatever is wrong with him was wrong with him before you married," I said, "and yet you married him. Nobody made you marry him, but something *inside of you* apparently made you ignore the inner stirrings of your spirit and marry him anyway. Did you think he would change? Better yet, that *you* could change him? You didn't make him cheat, but you may have contributed to your own pain by ignoring the still, small Voice within you.

"You needed to be married, but I'll bet you were never really comfortable with him. You made a decision, took a gamble, and it backfired. Now you're angry with him and you have a right to be, but aren't you also a little angry with yourself?"

By this time, I thought she was going to walk out of my office. She was so angry she was trembling.

"Why are you saying these things to me?" she asked.

"Because," I said, "if you keep on blaming him for everything, you're never going to heal. Every time you think of his wrong behavior, you're going to get angrier. You're going to talk to someone who's going to pat you on the back and tell you how justified you are for being angry, and in the process, you're going to separate yourself farther and farther from God. That anger will block out the power of God's spirit to heal you. And even though you're not thinking that you need God's spirit now, I'm here to tell you that you do, or at least you will."

I paused, then said, "Acknowledge your part so that you won't repeat the same behavior again."

Needless to say, this woman did no such thing that day. Right before she left, I told her that she was responsible for how she handled her hurt, just as she had been responsible for entering into a relationship and then a marriage that she knew wasn't right. "You acknowledge your part and then God gets to work on you," I said. "Right now, you want to do God's work. You want to be the judge. You want your husband to hurt like you hurt, and you want to inflict his pain, if at all possible, or at least make sure his life is miserable.

"But the task of dealing with your husband belongs to God. Unfortunately, you can't hurt or help your husband. You can only work on you."

It took a long time for the woman to come back to me. I didn't give her a teaspoon of sugar water, but a bitter taste of what life in the Lord is really all about. Eventually, she did come back to talk.

"What am I supposed to do?" she asked. "How do I acknowledge my part when all my energy has been spent on hating and blaming him?" Now we could begin.

Forgive Who?

꒰ꞏꞏ꒱

True forgiveness can't happen until we begin to acknowledge our roles in our own painful experiences. We actively lash out or passively choose to continue to hurt. In preparation for a recent Bible class, I read that Jesus admonished people not to hold anger in their hearts. A murderer breaks the Law for sure, Jesus said, but a person who is angry with another person is *just as guilty as a murderer.* (Matthew 5:21–22) Jesus says that both the murderer and the one who harbors anger are subject to the same judgment from God.

The Greek word for anger used in this scripture is *orge*, and it describes anger that has festered and caused bitterness in one's soul. A person feeds this type of anger and won't let it die. This type of anger is fed feelings of justification in order to keep it alive. We're not allowed to harbor that kind of anger, no matter what's been done to us or how bad it was.

As I write this, I think of African Americans and Jewish people. Both groups have been unjustly treated and history acknowledges it. No one deserved to be enslaved or gassed to death. If you ask an African American or a Jew to acknowledge his or her part in history, you'd be hurling an insult and you probably wouldn't get an answer. Yet, they have played a part, maybe not in the events that affected their people, but in the way they responded to those events. By incubating the pain, they've decided to remain in pain. The psychic ache experienced by both groups after the fact looms larger than the actual torment.

The same holds true for a parent whose child was murdered. It's true that both child and parents are victims. Still, Jesus would ask, "What has been your part in all of this? How did you respond to the pain?" If the parents can't let go and are hell-bent on seeking revenge against the murderer, Christianity might seem a worthless and insensitive religion. Yet, how has an eye for an eye helped us? The teachings of the Christ—forgiveness, forgetting, turning the other cheek, and true repentance—offer the strongest hope for healing individuals, societies, and nations.

Acknowledging our role in the events that hurt us is a hard thing to do. What if, for example, parents neglected to set a curfew for their teen. The teen stays out too late and is hurt. In order to heal, the parents must acknowledge their role in what happened. Sometimes our pain is caused by decisions we make and don't make. Refusing to look at ourselves keeps us from growing and healing.

We must also acknowledge how we feel about what's happened to us. When we're in pain, we don't want to hear about our role in the event. But if we can view forgiveness as God's way of healing our own souls versus affecting change in others, then acknowledging our role in continuing the pain is a first and necessary step.

God holds up a mirror to us, not to punish us but to enlighten us. God doesn't want us to hurt. He wants us to see what He sees all the time—children who sometimes mess up but who are worthy of His love and attention nonetheless. Such self-knowledge erases self-righteousness and makes us pray harder and look for a way out, thus releasing the venom we hold inside ourselves. The more venom we release, the more room we have for God's healing spirit. No matter how devastating the pain, we learn first-hand that God's power is greater.

How does this work when evil is done to us or to those we love? How does this work when forces, powers, and principalities have wreaked havoc without regard to the toll upon our souls? What do we acknowledge when a child is murdered or raped, when a people, like the Jews or African Americans, are systematically brutalized and dehumanized? How do we stop blaming others so that we can see how to change ourselves and our response to pain?

Most of us have seen the picture of a young Vietnamese girl running naked and screaming with other children after their village had been napalmed. The photo was taken during the Vietnamese War and won a Pulitzer Prize. This girl, now a young woman, survived 17 operations and was at one point paraded in Vietnam for propaganda purposes against the United States. In essence, she has suffered immensely. Surely, she was a victim. She had nothing to do with the war and what people did to her in the course of that war. She had no choice but to undergo the surgeries and bear the humiliation of her mutilated body being smeared all over her country's media.

Yet, she decided she didn't want to nurse the anger. She left Vietnam, and after studying in Moscow, she decided to become a missionary. She let the anger out. In order to do that, she had to acknowledge that she was holding the anger in, to her own detriment. From extreme brokenness she has become whole, or is at least closer to being whole than she was before.[1]

When I was a child, I saved up money to buy my mother some perfume. I didn't know what kind of perfume she liked, but I'd seen a bottle with a shape and color that titillated me; so I purchased it for her Mother's Day present.

She didn't like it. She didn't like the fragrance, and she told me so. I was bitterly stung and hurt. My mother never wore the perfume. The beautiful bottle stayed on top of the China cabinet in the dining room for weeks, until one day I sadly threw it away, sobbing the whole time.

Such a little thing, and yet for me it was major. For years, I held onto the pain. Then one day after reading about forgiveness, I could hear God ask me, "What was your part?"

At first I balked. I was a kid. I had good intentions. I saved my money to get it. I gave a slew of excuses that absolved me from wrongdoing.

God's voice was insistent. "What was your part?" I finally had to admit that I could have asked my mom or someone else what kind of perfume she liked. I purchased the perfume for no other reason than the shape of the bottle. My mother's likes or dislikes hadn't factored into my decision making. That was my role in my own pain. For years I'd been so self-righteous about the incident, but when I came to myself, I was able to let go of some of the deep anger and pain that had affected my relationship with my mother.

It's a difficult thing to do. I was faced with this dilemma recently while reading an account of how John Perkins, a civil rights leader, had been brutalized for helping African Americans to register to vote and for speaking out against police brutality. As I read about how white church-going folks had beaten this man senseless, made him mop up his own blood and then beaten him again before arresting him for inciting a riot, I could feel a familiar rush of resentment rise within me. There is no justification for abject evil. What, exactly, was I supposed to acknowledge?

That I was letting the reality of that evil control my emotions.

I could choose to remain stuck in my anger, or I could choose to give the pain to God. I didn't want to give it to God because I knew was right. It's true that what had been done to us was wrong. But more than the pain, anger, and self-righteousness, I realized that I want a free spirit and the ability to function in this society. If I hate all white people because of what some white people did, I'm the loser. So, I began to talk to myself and God, acknowledging my hitherto lack of willingness to let go of the anger, and began letting God move out the old spirit in order to make room for a new one.

A young woman spoke to me about her hatred of men. Relatives had molested her for a long time—from the age of three until the age of 11. All of the men had been churchmen, she said, and all of them had taught her that *she* was the bad one. She now hated men and she was angry with God. She made it a practice not to get too close to any man, though she's slept with many, and she's stayed clear of churches.

I asked her the hard question: "What has been your role in all of this?" This woman truly did get angry. The thought that she had anything at all to do with being molested was insulting, as well it should have been. But I wasn't asking her about what she did to cause the molestation. I was asking her about her role in deciding to believe men rather than God when they told her she was bad and responsible for her pain. I was asking about her decision to spend her life "getting back" at her tormentors by being promiscuous and rejecting commitment. I was asking about her decision to spend her life trying to hurt all men because of what a few men had done to her.

"Someone hurt you a long time ago," I said, "but you decided to make the hurt last. That's the 'your part' I'm talking about. If you could trust God enough now to give Him your hurt and the memory of it, you'd feel differently."

Put that way, it's hard to argue. We don't like hearing this

perspective, but it really is true. Then we ask, "But *why* did God le
it happen?" Unfortunately, we may never know. What we do get is a
sense of peace despite what happened to us. While most of us say we
want peace, too often we choose spiritual chaos and unrest because
we refuse to acknowledge our roles in our pain.

Forgive Who?

❧❧❧

Ultimately it doesn't matter what the unnamed son did in the story
of the Prodigal Son (Luke 15:11–32). What matters is that whatever
he did—run away from home, squander his inherited fortune, dis
respect his father—it wasn't enough to gain him the permanent en
mity of his father. The so-called prodigal was not a bad person, but
he'd certainly made some serious mistakes.

The elder son, also unnamed, was the so-called "good boy"
who became angry when the younger son did not, in his estimation
get what was coming to him for his wayward behavior. After having
been gone for too long, worrying his father to a state of grief, this
hooligan just shows up. That was bad enough, but when his father
welcomed him back with open arms, asking the servants to prepare
a feast and get him fine clothes, it was too much.

The elder son wasn't happy that his brother had returned home
or that he was alright. He felt anger and resentment because his father
apparently had no sense of justice. The younger son, in his brother's
opinion, needed to earn his way back into everyone's good graces
But no, he just walked back in and took up where he had left off.

When I read this story, it occurs to me that the younger brother
had taken stock of his behavior. It would have been easy for him to
blame his father for his behavior. Perhaps, he could have said the
father never understood him or was too hard on him. Or maybe the
father wouldn't let him express his individuality. Maybe the father
had been too hell-bent on his son following in his footsteps, and the
younger son just didn't want to do that. Or maybe the father, out
of frustration, had always picked on him. Maybe there was just no
peace between the two of them, and in desperation, the younger son
had taken off. Kids have a way of justifying their behavior, no matter
what the truth of the matter is.

There came a point in this young man's sojourn when he was so hungry that he wanted to "fill his stomach with the pods the pigs were eating." (Luke 15:16) At some point, he apparently stopped blaming his father, family, and all others, and took ownership of his predicament. The Bible says he "came to his senses" and set out to put his life back in order. (Luke 15:18)

While he stood in the pigs' pen, he smelled their stench and his own. He realized that no matter what reasons he had conjured up as justification for his leaving home, he had some part in it. When we come to our senses, we're finally in a place to consider what part we might have played in the situation. This may have happened to the younger son.

The elder son saw no need to come to his senses. He was filled with self-righteousness. He'd done no wrong. In fact, during the absence of his younger brother, he'd gone overboard to show his father his love and loyalty. In his estimation, his efforts had meant nothing. The father, ignoring him as he welcomed the younger son home, seemed not to care about what the elder boy was feeling or about all the work he had done to make his father's life easier while the younger son was away. He was so angry he

> "refused to go in. So his father went out and pleaded with him. But he answered his father, 'Look! All these years I have been slaving for you and never disobeyed your orders. Yet you never gave me even a young goat so I could celebrate with my friends. But when this son of yours who has squandered your property with prostitutes comes home, you kill the fatted calf for him!'" (Luke 15:28–30)

Anyone would be angry and resentful. It really wasn't fair, the way the younger son just eased back into his father's life. But he came back different, if the Scriptures are to be believed. He came back repentant, humble, aware of what he'd done and how wrong it had been. The elder son probably thought it was an act to get back into his father's good graces and that the younger probably disrespected his father for being such a chump as to fall for it all. We feel the same way when a convict is "converted" while in prison. We don't recognize or respect such conversions and regard them as convenient manipulations of the hearts and emotions of people who have the power to set them free.

So, the elder son was skeptical of the younger son's *mea culpa* But what he didn't do was acknowledge his response of resentment and anger to the situation. It was his choice to feel this way. He de
cided to give in to the resentment and anger rather than deciding that, fair or not, he was not going to react in a way that would be unpleasing to God. In fact, God's desires weren't even considered. He seldom is when self-righteousness is driving our behavior.

Self-righteousness was killing the elder son spiritually, though he didn't know it and wouldn't have admitted it if he had known it. In fact, as the younger brother returned from physical exile, the elder went out into a spiritual exile from his family and God. Who could blame him for his anger? His feelings were justified. Forgiving his brother was out of the question, and so was admitting his role in his own pain. As long as he believed that his brother deserved to be punished, he would stay stuck in a childish sibling grudge.

The important takeaway in this story is that the wayward son experienced peace despite his many mistakes while the model child probably died in spiritual and emotional anguish because of his self righteousness and refusal to forgive his father for being so generous to his brother. I believe that the younger son experienced peace because he acknowledged his role in the pain he felt and was able to somehow forgive himself and move on. The older son couldn't acknowledge his role in his own pain, and he grew increasingly bitter and angry.

Compared to his older brother, the younger son was obviously a sinner. He was carefree, careless, and irresponsible. I doubt he went to the temple regularly, and when he did, it was under duress. This young man rebelled against authority and wouldn't listen to anyone except the voice of his own incessant wants and needs. He didn't respect his father or his brother, nor did he meet his family responsi bilities. He took life and love for granted. He put more faith in money and possessions than in family and faith. Surely, he was destined for trouble and adversity.

His elder brother, on the other hand, probably said his prayers every night. He probably sang in the temple, and his good behavior made everyone nod in approval at his Bar Mitzvah. He did as he was told, and then some. He lived to please others, especially his family and specifically his father. He shunned the fast life and stayed close to home. Undoubtedly, he believed he was in line for great things because of his model behavior.

When his younger brother took off, the elder son worked even harder to please his distraught father. It bothered him that despite his best efforts, his father seemed not to love the younger son less. How many nights had the elder son spent trying to get his father to forget the young troublemaker and be thankful for the dutiful son he still had? Ah, he thought. "My father will soon forget this rogue."

But the father didn't forget him. The elder son continued to try to please his father more. When his tired father would come back home after searching for and not finding his son, this model son may have met him at the door and tried to comfort him. If it bothered him, he didn't dare show it. To show such a thing would have exposed him for being less than "a good boy," and in no shape or fashion did he want to reveal himself in that light.

As time went on, his father seemed to be coming around until the fateful day when he heard his father shout. At first, he didn't know why his father's voice could be heard over the sounds of the day. Could he have been attacked? Were the flocks okay? The older son's heart raced as he rushed toward his father's voice.

"It's my son!" the father cried aloud. "He's come home! Come! It's my son!"

The older son stewed as he watched his father's face become streaked with tears of joy, and his stomach turned when his father ran out to meet his brother. Already, he was in a place that was going to prevent, or at least make difficult the process of forgiveness. Already, he was refusing to admit his role in his own feelings.

He grew angry as he watched his father embrace and kiss his brother. *He actually kissed him!* After all he'd done. When he was asked to get not only a robe, but the best robe for his brother, asked to put a ring on his finger and to prepare a feast, it was more than the elder son could handle. Being the dutiful, model son he was, he obeyed, but inside he burned with anger and probably hatred.

Thus, one brother received salvation while the other doomed himself to emotional and spiritual torment. Not being able or willing to acknowledge our role in our pain is a huge barrier that prevents us from even beginning the process of forgiveness. It's the most difficult step of the entire process because we can't lay complete blame on the other guy. That takes away a sense of our power and righteousness, and self-righteousness is a necessary component of an unforgiving spirit.

Forgive Who?

⁂

Even as I write this, I have to admit that what's good for the goose is good for the gander. If the truth be told, there are some gaping holes in my ability to acknowledge my part in some of my pain and issues I, too, have found it easier to replay what they did to me, rather than consider what I may have done to contribute to a situation. I've also had to come to terms with the fact that in deciding to be angry and resentful at times, I've contributed to my own pain.

What to do? Unfortunately, there's no quick road to the place of forgiveness. We're reluctant travelers because the road is so rough It's tempting to turn back and stay in anger and pain just as the Israelites reconsidered Egyptian slavery. (Exodus 14:12) In their frustration the Israelites forgot that the wilderness journey was necessary for deliverance, for freedom. So is forgiveness. In our frustration we say, "Forget this forgiveness business! It's too hard! And I'm not sure it's worth it!"

But it is. Deliverance is always worth it. When one has a bad back, the pain of surgery is worth the relief once the incision has healed. When a leg is broken, the pain of getting the leg set is worth it once that bone heals. If the broken leg is not reset, it will heal badly, and the result will be a lifetime of pain and discomfort, just because we didn't want to go through the necessary steps to healing. I recently read that white women get breast cancer more often than do African American women, but that more African Americans die from it because they get treatment too late. Men needlessly die of diseases because they don't want to get regular checkups.

Likewise, we're reluctant to do what's necessary to heal spiritually. When the road gets rough, we're apt to give up, much less even begin the process. If part of that journey is giving up blaming others and asking ourselves what part we've played, many of us will just stop the journey and like the Israelites, opt for slavery to a pain that does not have to be. Instead of praying for strength at those difficult times, too many of us just throw in the towel.

I can hear some of you protesting. For those who have been *Acknowledging* grievously wronged, like being raped or molested, or for those who *Your Part* have suffered the loss of loved ones, your protests are noted. You didn't cause the situation, but you are perpetuating your own misery. You must begin to realize that your pain persists because you won't let it go. Holding on to the pain separates you from the healing that God wants you to have *right now.*

The painful truth of the matter is this: If we don't confront our own feelings, our own barriers, and admit the part we're playing in keeping a bad situation alive, we'll be forever caught in a cycle of resentment, anger, and pain that won't get better but instead will deepen over time.

Our desire to be close to God should inspire us to acknowledge our role in all situations. It's not a weakness to acknowledge our issues before God. This confession will prove to be our strength and a positive action we can take to keep us in a strong relationship with God.

Acknowledging our role in our pain shows a willingness to trust God with our most delicate feelings. We're believing that whatever God has for us on the other side of the wilderness is a lot better than where we are right now.

Questions for Study

1. Why is acknowledging our role in the perpetuation of our own pain so difficult?
2. Discuss a situation that was so painful that you can't even begin to consider your role at all.
3. What do you have to lose by acknowledging your part? What do you have to gain?
4. Discuss the story of the prodigal son. Do you identify yourself with the younger son or the elder?

5. How do you interpret the scriptural phrase "came to himself?" Is that something you want to do? Why or why not?

6. Is it necessary for ethnic or other minority groups to acknowledge their roles in their own oppression? Why might they protest such an idea?

7. Oppressors remain oppressive because they don't acknowledge their role in any of their actions. For example, many in America are reluctant to admit that racism is as bad as it is. They're reluctant to admit the government's role in the perpetuation of racism. How can the world change if oppressors never acknowledge their actions?

Chapter 9
The Real Issue

O LORD, YOU DECEIVED ME, AND I WAS DECEIVED; YOU OVERPOWERED
ME AND PREVAILED. I AM RIDICULED ALL DAY LONG; EVERYONE MOCKS ME.
WHENEVER I SPEAK, I CRY OUT PROCLAIMING VIOLENCE AND DESTRUCTION.
SO THE WORD OF THE LORD HAS BROUGHT ME INSULT AND REPROACH ALL
DAY LONG."
–JEREMIAH 20:7–8

In the play *Aida*, the two main characters, Aida, a Nubian princess who has been captured by Egyptians, and Radames, her captor, fall in love. It wasn't planned. In fact, it was quite unheard of that an Egyptian would consider a Nubian to be anything other than a slave. Egyptians and Nubians were enemies.

But the two fall in love, much to the chagrin and discomfort of them both. Aida has been assigned to serve as the personal handmaiden of Amneris, Pharaoh's daughter, who is also in love with Radames. The situation is further complicated by Radames' father, who is slowly poisoning the Pharaoh so Radames can be the new ruler of Egypt. In order to rule, Radames must marry Amneris, to whom he has been betrothed for years.

Meanwhile, Aida's father is captured by Radames' men and the impossibility of her ever hoping to be with Radames becomes apparent to the princess. Aida tells Radames that he must marry Amneris the next day as has been planned. He says he'll honor her request and also make sure her father isn't killed. In turn, he asks her to return to Nubia and never come back so that he'll not be in anguish over not being able to have her. They profess their undying love for each other and proceed to do as they have planned.

Unknown to both of them, Amneris has heard their entire conversation and is heartbroken. She knows that they both will have to be killed—Radames for committing treason by cavorting with the enemy and Aida for no other reason than she is Nubian and has stepped into forbidden territory. The marriage takes place as planned, and right after the two have said their vows, word comes to the palace that Aida's father has escaped. It becomes clear that Radames helped him. Pharaoh orders his death and Aida's. They will be buried alive, according to the Egyptian law which designates how traitors are to die. They will be killed separately, he decrees.

Now Amneris steps forward. Still heartbroken because her husband must die and because she knows he doesn't love her, she intervenes, telling her father that they both know he's on the brink of death ("there is poison in your veins," Amneris reminds him) and that she, as heir to the throne, will be the next ruler of Egypt. She asks her father if the two lovers can be buried together.

Pharaoh gasps, "But that would be mercy!"[1]

Amneris knows it, but tells her father that she has the authority to make the decision and she decrees that they will die together. She is not bitter; she is sad, because she knows they love each other and want to be together. Since they cannot be together in life, she allows them to have their last few hours of life together.

Truly, it comes off as an act of mercy, forgiveness in its finest form.

Pharaoh didn't want to forgive. His cry, "But that would be mercy!" is a cry to which we can all relate. When we've been wronged more than not being able to forgive, we usually just don't want to. We view forgiveness as a sign of weakness rather than strength, and in our pain, we seek to redefine our position. Forgiveness, or the mere thought of it, gets in the way.

Yet, it's the only remedy for freeing ourselves from the pain we feel from being wronged.

In his book *Forgive and Forget*, Lewis B. Smedes says that there are four stages of forgiving: hurting, hating, healing ourselves, and coming together. He says that forgiving seems unnatural; we wonder if there's a payoff and we cry out that it isn't fair.[2] Yet, it's the only salve for a hurt that gnaws at us all the day long. The reason forgiveness works to free us, Smedes explains, is because it helps us to rediscover the humanity of the person who hurt us. It makes us surrender our right to get even, and it helps us revise our feelings

112

toward the person we forgive. In essence, Smedes is telling us to bless our enemies.[3]

That's well and good, but too few of us are interested in forgiveness and close to none want to bless their enemies. That's unnatural and, some would argue, not even required by God. We ignore the words of scripture that say, "Love your enemies and pray for those who persecute you." (Matthew 5:44) Some have argued that Jesus didn't even give that command and that some do-gooder added the words later.

As I write this, I think of the family of Laci Peterson, the pregnant woman who disappeared from her home on Christmas Eve, 2002. Her body and that of her baby were found months later in the water near San Francisco, and the husband was arrested for the crime. Would not the parents of Laci slap me (and maybe justifiably so) if I suggested to them that they are bound to forgive whomever killed their daughter? Moreover, would I be willing to even listen to such nonsense if it were *my* daughter and grandchild?

What Jesus asks of us is not easy. It's not meant to be. But we learn that Jesus only asks the impossible of us *for our own good*. It helps me, at least, to know that if I *were* in the Peterson's situation, I would not be required to have tea and crumpets with the murderer. Nor would I be in danger of casting myself into hell if I desired justice for the wrong done. Forgiving does not mean that we can't want justice. Any murderer must answer for his or her crime. But as a Christian, I am commanded by Jesus to forgive the person and leave the justice issues to those who can properly mete them out.

Jeremiah, the prophet, complained to God that although he was doing as God had commanded, he had no peace. Jeremiah was called to be a prophet when he was very young. God spoke to him, saying, "Before I formed you in the womb I knew you, before you were born I set you apart; I appointed you as a prophet to the nations." (Jeremiah 1:5)

Jeremiah protested, saying he was only a child and didn't know how to speak, but God spoke back and advised Jeremiah not to worry. Do not say, 'I am only a child.' You must go to everyone I send you to and say whatever I command you. Do not be afraid of them, for I am with you and will rescue you." (Jeremiah 1:7–8)

Jeremiah tried to obey God, but despite hearing from the prophet "what thus saith the Lord," the people wouldn't listen. They disobeyed God. They also gave Jeremiah a hard time. They insulted, reproached, and ignored him.

It hurt. They didn't care about Jeremiah, nor did they heed his message of "do right or perish" the way Jeremiah thought they should have. Instead of repenting, they became more belligerent, stubborn, and resistant. They didn't believe Jeremiah was so special that his revelations were more profound than those received by the other priests. It was as though they believed what he was telling them was just his opinion, and they rejected much of what he said.

Jeremiah was mad at God and the people. He might have been able to let the people off the hook. After all, they were mere mortals. But God was God! God was supposed to go before him and make the road a little easier. God was supposed to grant Jeremiah a reward as payment for his trouble. He hadn't asked to be a preacher or prophet. God had approached him! Couldn't God have provided more support and a more receptive and larger audience for his salvation and deliverance message?

Why were the people so rebellious? Why hadn't God warned him how the people would respond, or at least given him the ability to handle it? His emotions were being ripped apart! After all, he was only human. He wanted to be heard, respected, and liked. Didn't God know how he felt? The constant barrage of insults and ridicule, not to mention being ignored, were making the job just too difficult.

Jeremiah didn't want to be a prophet anymore. He didn't want to preach, either.

He wasn't endeared to the people he was charged to save, nor they to him. Far from it. He was angry, hurt, and betrayed by both God and the people. Truth be told, he didn't care whether they lived or died.

That's what injustice, unfairness, and cruelty can do to us. That's how we feel when bad things happen to us through no fault of our own. We do the best we can and still, the situation doesn't get better.

That's when we want revenge. Hang forgiveness.

Recently, I watched a young man testify at his father's trial. The father had been accused of killing the young man's mother. As I listened to him painfully recount conversations he'd had with his father, I wondered what he was thinking and feeling. Could he forgive his father for committing such a horrible crime? If this had happened to me, could I forgive? It seemed like a good time to talk to God about it, so I asked Him, "Lord, are you saying he has to forgive his father, the man who murdered his mother?" God answered in the affirmative. I asked aloud, "How can You expect that?" He was characteristically silent. I knew by His silence it was one of "those questions" that I was bound to deal with until I gained understanding.

The Real Issue

On another program, a mother talked about how a bounty hunter murdered her son in front of her eyes, even though the son was not wanted for anything and hadn't done anything. I kept asking myself, "What would I have done in that situation?" What would forgiveness even look like in that situation?

These types of situations make us ask God, "Why would You even give us something so *inhuman* to do?" We are repulsed by the thought of forgiving because we don't understand what is required. Smedes argues that forgiving is completely human; we are freeing ourselves, after all. Where we go wrong is that we think forgiveness means we *tolerate* and maybe even *excuse* what was done to us.[4] It doesn't mean that. In fact, if forgiveness is going to work at all, we have to be honest with ourselves and with the person against whom we hold a grudge. We don't have to pretend like nothing ever happened. When we're honest, we let go of resentment. It's a fact that if we can't be honest about the situation, we'll never be able to forgive!

So, God wants us to want personal healing. He wants us to crave a cleansing that will set us free. If we think about it that way, the notion of forgiveness is a bit easier to swallow.

Doing a "heart check" actually helps us know if we've forgiven or not. In some situations, I've been successful at forgiving, and in other areas, not so successful. I have to admit that in some cases I'm more interested in protecting myself than with doing God's will and trusting Him to nurse me back to health. When a young girl in my congregation hurt my feelings a number of years ago, I went through the beginning stages of forgiveness—you know, allowing that she was a human being and a young one at that. But somewhere in the process, I must have stopped because to this day I still harbor resentment toward her. I don't know if I'm trying to let go of the feelings, either. I know God wants me to want to be healed of the pain, but my actions and lingering resentment let me know that I've decided that I don't want the healing, at least not yet.

That brings us to a very important part of the process of *wanting* to forgive. In order for the desire to forgive to take precedence over the tendency to hold onto hurt feelings, we must realize that there are aspects of ourselves that God requires us to relinquish. We must efface ourselves for the process of forgiveness to be effective.

A member of my congregation was angry with me one Holy Season because at our Holy Thursday service I washed the feet of the choir. In our church, in addition to pastoring I had been choir director for years, because we didn't have a director. I worked hard with and for the choir, but often didn't feel respected by them. I had no idea others in the congregation felt that lack of respect as well.

Anyway, this particular Holy Season, I was convicted that God had commanded me to wash their feet. Up to that year, I had only washed the feet of the deacons. When I heard God command me to wash the feet of the choir, my heart sank. I didn't want to do it. I realized as I had this conversation with God that I had been harboring anger and resentment for a while.

I was obedient. I washed their feet. As I washed their feet, I sobbed and said with each one, "The Son of Man did come not to be served, but to serve." (Matthew 20:28) It was, frankly, humiliating but I knew I had to do it.

When the footwashing portion of the service was over, I noticed that one of my members got up and walked out. The next day she called me and said, "I was mad at you for washing their feet. They didn't deserve it. I couldn't have done it."

Well, she was right. *She* couldn't have done it. I hadn't done it. The spirit of God in me had done what I could never have done on my own. I had to lose all my pride. My member continued, "It made me look at the footwashing thing (that's how she said it) differently

Up until last night, I didn't think that anyone would have been mad at Jesus for washing feet, but now I don't know. I'll bet somebody was mad at Jesus, standing over at the side wall wondering why Jesus would even wash the feet of some whom *they* thought didn't deserve it. That means Jesus had to forgive all the dumb stuff they had done and the mean stuff (meaning Judas) they were about to do."

She paused and then went on. "No, it's even deeper. That meant He had to wash Peter's feet when He knew he was going to deny Him. He had to forgive Thomas even though he wouldn't recognize Him after He died, in spite of having the evidence of the crucifixion. I don't like this at all," she said.

And yet, she admitted, she was finally beginning to *see* what forgiveness was all about. "You can't be proud and forgive someone," she said, "and I've got to tell you. I am not there."

She was honest, but she "got it." Forgiveness requires us to lose some of ourselves so that we can receive a greater good, namely freedom from pain. We gain new life and begin to see what Jesus meant when he said, "Whoever wants to save his life will lose it, but whoever loses his life for me will find it." (Matthew 16:25) We find a new relationship with Jesus the Christ, a new freedom, a new release from things that have held us captive.

In addition to pride, there are other things we're required to relinquish if forgiveness is going to work. There's fear—of being perceived as a weakling and of being hurt again.

There's the tendency to judge the other person as being bad. All of us have wronged someone from time to time, and we don't consider ourselves bad. Our tendency to judge others really blocks the work of forgiveness.

There's the desire to hold onto our victimization. We have to relinquish our desire to be a victim. Holding onto being a victim for the sake of justifying our resentment is an absolute deterrent to being able to forgive.

To enter into the process of forgiveness requires that we let go of our raw (justified) emotions and know this will help us. God wants us to want a relationship with Him more than we want to get someone back for hurting us.

All of this is what taking up the cross and following Him

means. (Luke 9:23) God never said it would be easy. When Jesus carried that heavy cross up the hill, his captors may have believed He was weakened, but we know that carrying the cross and succumbing to it ultimately strengthened Him because he was honoring his relationship with God. Carrying our crosses strengthens our relationship with God and crucifies the things we must relinquish in order to experience a resurrected spirit. It's not easy, but it's necessary.

As a pastor, I've had to learn to force myself to enter into the process of forgiveness more than once. What amazes me is how taking up the cross of forgiveness, which is hard and gnarly to bear really does in the long run release me from the burden of pain. It doesn't make human sense, it isn't logical, but it works.

❧❧❧

One of the members of my church really couldn't stand me. I didn't know it, but she spent a lot of time putting me down and talking about me pretty badly. When I found out what she'd been saying, I said nothing, absorbed the pain, and generally tried to stay out of her way.

Then one day I received a call. This member had been rushed to the hospital. She was very sick with terminal colon cancer.

Whew! That was a hard one. I felt badly for her, but not really sad. That was my hurt humanity working. But as her pastor, I knew I had to go to see her. *I didn't want to go.* I was tempted to send a deacon, but it was as though the Lord Himself put His hand on my shoulder. I knew I had to go. I was the pastor, and for whatever reason, this woman called me.

After Sunday service, I went straight to the hospital. Tense the whole time, tears rolled down my cheeks. I was mad that I had to do this. I railed at God, asking him why He had put me in this position. Why couldn't He send someone else? Why, as a matter of fact, had He called me to this stupid job? I knew I was in trouble. The only way I'd be able to minister to this lady would be to forgive her. She had called for me, and I had to go. I'd have to let go of my hurt feelings because she needed me.

It's called denying yourself and taking up your cross.

When I got to the hospital, every step toward her room was painful. I kept telling God that I couldn't do it. He never gave me permission to stop moving toward her. When I got outside of her room, I froze. I could hear her voice and the voices of her sons. "Great," I told God, "You've got me walking into a cesspool of dislike." I knew she hadn't kept her dislike of me a secret from her sons.

I felt the tears coming again, but it was like God shook me. I lowered my head and walked in. For a moment, there was an uncomfortable silence. "I can run out now and nobody will be the worse for it," I pleaded with God. He didn't respond. As I walked toward her bed, I muttered under my breath, "Create in me a pure heart, O God, and renew a steadfast spirit within me." (Psalm 51:10) I didn't want to lift my head. I didn't want to look at her. I didn't want to touch her. But I had to. I was her pastor.

When I got to her bedside and looked into her eyes, I couldn't believe how God had lifted the burden from me. Don't get me wrong. I wasn't completely comfortable, but the angst and pain I felt outside her door were gone. When I looked into her eyes, I could see *her* pain and *her* fear. I don't think she thought I was going to come. And, of course, she was right. Had I not heard from God to "go," I would have sent someone else. There was a reason for all of this; I knew it as I looked into her eyes. Impulsively, I hugged her. That was God working. The tears were streaming down her face, and she held onto my hand as tightly as anyone ever has.

I couldn't say much because God was working too hard on *me*, so I merely gathered the family around her bed. We held hands and prayed. Before I left, her oldest son gave me a hug. God was telling me that He really did have the situation under control.

I got through that experience. I entered into the process, not because I wanted to, but because I had to. I'm not sure that I would have even visited her if I hadn't been the pastor. My human "you got what you deserved" mantra might have kicked in. I hope not, but the possibility was there. I didn't want to forgive. I didn't want to let go of my justified hurt feelings, but I was forced to. Once I entered the process, God took over.

And I realized something. One of the biggest reasons we don't want to forgive is because we really don't *trust* that God will take over and take care of us. In addition, if the truth be told, we really don't want Him to. We'd rather hurt because what Jesus demands is too difficult and too distasteful. I read in Philip Yancey's latest book, *Soul Survivor,* that Leo Tolstoy and Feodor Dostoevsky spent a lifetime trying to really follow Jesus. They, like us, found the path difficult and sometimes discouraging. Yancey concludes that "to follow Jesus does not mean to solve every human problem ... but rather to respond as he did, against all reason, to dispense grace and love to those who deserve it least."[5]

Forgive Who?

In the long run, forgiving someone is easier than holding onto the garbage. It's easier spiritually, emotionally, and physically to love someone and risk being thought of as a chump than to carry around unresolved issues. When I fail to forgive, my whole system reacts negatively. I get grumpy, moody, and prone to headaches and other aches. Instead of moving forward, I focus too much attention on watching what the other guy's next move will be.

When I'm able to let go and let God, I find an amazing freedom. It doesn't matter to me what is done, said, or thought about me. When I met, face to face, a former deaconess who led the insurrection against me years ago, I felt no pain or anger. I could hug her and move on. That's only the Lord. When the Lord directed me to hug my ex-husband's second wife (which I did after some rigorous protests), I again felt nothing. She was about to leave the country and I had taken my children over to say goodbye to her. As I sat in my car waiting for them to hug each other, I heard God say to me, "Get out and go hug her." I *immediately* said no! But in spite of my protests God prevailed and I ended up hugging her. I was okay. It was amazing. I felt nothing. No anger, nothing. In fact, that process with the second wife had begun two years earlier when I asked my kids if they wanted to get her a Christmas present. She'd been nice to them as a stepmother, and I appreciated it. We got her a music box, and I felt no anger or pain. I wasn't afraid that she'd think me weak. When she called me on Christmas day, crying out of gratitude, I honestly didn't know what to say.

There's something powerful and miraculous about being able to forgive someone against all reason. Unfortunately, the church doesn't concentrate on forgiveness enough, probably because it's too ard and too distasteful even for men and women of the cloth.

Still, Jesus requires us to forgive one another because God forgives all of us. When we step out of line, God doesn't pick and choose who will receive his love, forgiveness, and grace. He doesn't rate our sins or kick to the curb those whose sin is "not so bad" in human eyes. Paul says in Romans that "God does not show favoritism." (Romans 2:11) If we're to believe the Bible, God forgives us all, no matter what we've done.

I know some Christians don't buy that. How many times have I heard Christians say that God won't forgive some sins, and then they carefully lay out their list of "unforgivable" sins. God forgives us all, no matter what. If I'm to believe the Bible and what Jesus said, then Jesus forgave Judas, Peter, Thomas, and those who crucified Him. He forgave thieves and murderers. If Jeffrey Dahmer repented, I have to believe God forgave him no matter how uncomfortable that makes me feel. If the white people who lynched innocent black people repented, I have to believe they were forgiven. If the Enron executives repent, I have to believe God will forgive them. If the snipers who terrorized Washington, DC, in late 2002 repent, I have to believe they will be forgiven. I might not like it, but it's the truth.

Jesus asks us what right we have *not* to forgive since God forgives all kinds of acts. On the one hand it might make you angry, but on the other hand, it should give you a sense of relief. Were it not for divine forgiveness, a whole lot of us would be in big trouble right now.

Jesus never said following His commands would be easy. He just said do these things. The payoff is being able to experience joy and liberation while we are alive. It's a gift that God wants us all to have. I think it's salvation in the flesh. God wants us to experience joy, not lead lives of quiet desperation filled with pain and anger.

He wants us to want joy more than we want to hurt, which means we've got to somehow talk ourselves into wanting to forgive.

Questions for Study

. Is there anyone that you don't want to forgive? Write down any and all names.

2. Now, explain why you don't want to forgive this person.

3. How long have you held this grudge?

4. What do you have to gain by holding onto your grudge? What do you have to lose?

5. Have you ever thought about trying to make amends? What happened?

6. What do you think about Jesus' command to go to the person who has offended you and be reconciled?

7. Have you ever been forgiven by someone you hurt badly? How did you feel when this person forgave you?

8. Are you willing to let someone who hurt you experience your forgiveness of him or her?

9. What do you teach your children about forgiveness? Is it an important discussion in your house?

10. What do you think about God forgiving everyone? Do you think He does or does not? Do you think some people are so bad they can't be forgiven?

Chapter 10
Are There Any Exceptions to the Rule?

"Absalom never said a word to Amnon, either good or bad; he hated Amnon because he had disgraced his sister Tamar."
—2 Samuel 13:22

There are plenty of disturbing stories in the Bible, and one of the most disturbing is about the rape of a woman by her own brother.

The two people involved were Tamar and Amnon, daughter and son, respectively, of King David. It seems that Amnon had fallen hopelessly in love with Tamar, his sister. Despite being an eligible man in his father's kingdom, and certainly able to choose any woman he might have wanted, he clung to his desire for his sister.

Amnon languished in misery, until one day he had a conversation with his friend Jonadab, who gave Amnon a way to have what he wanted.

> "Go to bed and pretend to be ill," Jonadab said. "When your father comes to see you, say to him, 'I would like my sister Tamar to come and give me something to eat. Let her prepare the food in my sight so I may watch her and then eat it from her hand.'"
> (2 Samuel 13:5–6)

So, a desperate and lustful Amnon did just that. The unsuspecting Tamar came to her allegedly sick brother, concerned, and was more than willing to obey his requests. One can only imagine Amnon's impatience as he allowed her to complete her tasks while he watched her. When she was finished preparing his food, she tried to serve him, but he wouldn't take it. Instead, he asked her to send everyone from the room.

Still unsuspecting, Tamar did as she was asked. When the room was empty, Amnon said to his sister, "Bring the food here into my bedroom so I may eat from your hand." (vs. 10) Tamar did as she was asked, but when she got close enough to her brother for him to touch her, he grabbed her and demanded, "Come to bed with me, my sister." (vs. 11)

Forgive Who?

Tamar was stunned. She may have thought, "He's delusional. He must have a fever. I must forgive him because he's talking out of his mind." For a moment, she may have been able to make sense of a terribly horrible moment. But within seconds, she was able to see that he was not delusional at all. He was lucid and clear; his eyes were as she had never seen them before, mean and piercing. His hold on her arm was painful, and he only tightened his grip as she tried to wrench herself away. No, she decided. He was not delusional. Something was terribly, terribly wrong.

She protested. "Don't my brother! Don't do this!" She reminded him that he was the king's son after all, and that their father, David, could arrange for him to have any woman he wanted. "Don't do this!" she cried. She tried appealing to his sense of loyalty to her; they had always been close and he had always looked out for her. Surely, he had not forgotten his filial love and concern for her. "What about me? Where could I get rid of my disgrace?" (vs. 13)

But Amnon wouldn't be moved. The Bible simply says that he "refused to listen to her, and since he was stronger than she, he raped her." (vs. 14) That was bad enough. After the assault, Tamar lay dishonored, wounded spiritually, emotionally, and physically. She wanted to move, to run, but she couldn't. She was too hurt, on too many levels. She lay still and wept.

But then, just when she thought it couldn't get any worse, she heard her brother's voice. "Get up and get out!" His voice was strange, like she had never heard it before. It was cold and hard and distant. He talked to her like she was nothing. The Bible in fact says that after he raped her, he hated her. "In fact, he hated her more than he had loved her." (vs. 15)

"Get out!" he commanded her. Tears streaming down her face, she lifted her head from the floor and said, "No. I can't do that. Sending me away would be a greater wrong than you have already done to me!" (vs. 16) She was reminding him that a woman who lost her virginity before being properly betrothed would be considered unclean nworthy of any good man. Nobody would want her; her life as a woman in ancient Israelite society was ruined. Surely he could not have forgotten that, and surely, though he had raped her, he would remember his relationship to her and not cast her away as nothing! So she thought.

But he refused to listen to her and had his personal servant come. "Get this woman out of here and bolt the door after her." (vs. 7) Tamar, incredulous, walked away, tearing her richly ornamented robe and putting ashes on her head as she did so. She felt dirty and betrayed and angry and hurt and alone. Would she be expected to forgive her brother?

Are There Any Exceptions to the Rule?

Certainly, her other brother, Absalom, would say no. He would tell her or any well-meaning religious person that forgiveness is not necessary. He would remind her that she had been brutalized, humiliated, and transposed from a highly honored woman into a woman despised because of the selfish lust of her own brother. Absalom was one of the first to see her after she left her brother's chambers. When she saw him, she turned away. It was too much. She didn't want to talk about what had happened. She was too ashamed. Perhaps Absalom would think she had brought it on herself. Perhaps he would blame her and bring up how she, in his opinion, had been too flirtatious. She couldn't bear the thought, so when she saw Absalom, she turned away, but he rushed to her and encouraged her to tell him what had happened.

Sobbing, she finally broke down and told him the whole sordid story. Absalom was shocked. "Has that Amnon, your brother, been with you? Be quiet now, my sister; he is your brother. Don't take this thing to heart." (vs. 20) He held his shaking, sobbing, demoralized sister in his arms, trying to comfort her.

But know this: Absalom was mad. Forgiveness was not part of the equation. He invited Tamar to live in his house, "a desolate woman," the Bible says, but that wasn't the end of the story. Absalom never said a word to his brother, good or bad, but he hated Amnon because he had disgraced his sister. Two years later, Absalom had Amnon murdered. (vs. 29) Though Absalom fled, he did so with a sense of justification. Amnon had gotten what he deserved. Forgiveness be hanged!

In the face of horrendous crimes and circumstances in our lives, are there ever exceptions to the need or requirement to forgive? A recent Lifetime movie dealt with a young man who killed his mother-in-law during an apparent episode of sleepwalking. Needless to say, the family of the murdered woman was properly incensed and wanted him to pay. The catch to the story was that his wife, the daughter of the murdered woman, was caught between hating him and believing that his deed had been a fluke due to his sleepwalking. When she decided to forgive him and make room for the possibility of his story being true, her brother and sister disowned her. Was she supposed to forgive him?

Forgive Who?

Reginald Denny, a truck driver, was beaten by rioters in Los Angeles in April 1992. They were angry over the acquittal of white police officers caught on tape beating Rodney King. The rioters crushed Denny's skull. He had done nothing except show up in the wrong place at the wrong time, and was consequently stomped on and bashed with a brick and a hammer. He forgave his attackers. Was he supposed to do that?

A young man's wife hadn't been faithful to him. They'd been married for four years, and apparently, she had had at least two partners outside of their marriage. He found out about it, and they were divorced, but in my office, he sobbed and explained how much he still loved her and that he had forgiven her. Was he supposed to do that?

Archbishop Desmond Tutu and South African President Nelson Mandela formed and supported the Truth and Reconciliation Commission. People who had committed horrendous crimes against blacks in South Africa were allowed to testify before the Commission and some were granted amnesty for full confessions of their crimes. The premise was that no amount of revenge would be effective or helpful. The crimes had already been committed, and the goal was to move forward. Miraculously, the people of South Africa abided by the decisions of the Commission, though they had every right to rebel and protest. They chose to forgive. Were they supposed to do that?

Was Simon Weisenthal supposed to forgive that wounded SS soldier on behalf of all the Jews who had been tortured and murdered? In other words, are there exceptions to the expectation that we forgive? Aren't there some crimes, some situations that beg us to hold our ground and withhold our forgiveness?

Scriptures, Christian and otherwise, would say "no." Consider the following:

- Subvert anger by forgiveness. (Jainism. Samanasuttam 136)
- The best deed of a great man is to forgive and forget. (Islam (Shiite) Nahjul Balagha, Saying 201)
- Where there is forgiveness, there is God Himself. (Sikhism. Adi Granth, Shalok, Kabir, p. 1372)
- If you efface and overlook and forgive, then lo! God is forgiving, merciful. (Islam. Qur'an 64.14)
- The superior man tends to forgive wrongs and deals leniently with crimes. (Confucianism. I Ching 40:Release)
- If you are offering your gift at the altar and there remember that your brother has something against you, leave your gift there before the altar and go; first be reconciled to your brother and then come and offer your gift. (Christianity. Matthew 5: 23–34)
- The Day of Atonement atones for sins against God, not for sins against man, unless the injured person has been appeased. (Judaism. Mishnah. Yoma 8.9)
- Show endurance in humiliation and bear no grudge. (Taoism. Treatise on Response and Retribution.)
- Do not seek revenge or bear a grudge against one of your people, but love your neighbor as yourself; I am the LORD. (Judaism and Christianity. Leviticus 19:18)

It appears that many, if not all religions teach somewhere in their doctrine and dogma that forgiveness is a necessary component of life.

That being the case, it might make it easier for us if we remember that forgiveness is not for the benefit of the offender; it is for the well-being of the wounded and wronged. If we, the wronged, can desire to be loosed of the burden of having to be perpetually angry with someone more than we desire to see or seek vengeance, we put ourselves in a place of being able to consider the benefits to us.

It helps, I think, to remember that forgiving someone doesn't mean we condone what he or she has done. It doesn't take away our right to blame another person for a pain we've felt in our lives, as long as feelings of self-righteousness don't trap us. A person who has done wrong really does have to be held accountable. We have to understand, however, that the person isn't accountable to us. He or she is accountable to God.

Forgiving someone doesn't mean we have to restore the relationship that existed prior to the offense. A woman who has been abused by her husband can forgive him and acknowledge that he has a problem without remaining married to him or remarrying him. A person can forgive a son or daughter who steals and lies and acknowledge that the child has a problem without allowing that same child another opportunity to do the same things. Forgiving allows us to see other people, even those who have hurt us, as human beings with faults and not become swallowed up in our anger over their problems and issues. Forgiveness allows us to acknowledge to ourselves that we cannot change them, nor should we try. We know them for what they are and interact with them accordingly.

It's a little easier to forgive if we can think that way. I know, for example, that my friend who lies for no good reason at all will never change. His lies have hurt my feelings in the past, but no more. Another friend of mine asked me how I could talk with him at all, given how his lies have affected my life, but it really isn't a big deal. I know he's a liar. I know he's an intrinsically good person with a major flaw. I know what that flaw is, and so I don't believe anything he says. I can still have lunch with him. I can talk with him on the phone and even laugh. But I don't invest any confidence in him that I know is likely to be shattered. I no longer invest energy into remembering what he's done to me. My decision is to be his friend in the way I can be his friend. If he ever needs me, I'll be there for him. But he'll never be able to take me to the depths of pain again because I believed something he said to me which turned out to be untrue. Forgiveness has allowed me to see him as human, not as a bad person.

The alternative is perpetual misery, caused by a build-up

of bitterness, anger, and hatred. That build-up warps us; it keeps us from seeing God in the midst of bad things happening to us. It makes us reject not only the offender but others who might have been sent to us by God to help ease the pain. It taints our attitudes and our vision, makes us hyper-reactive and way too sensitive. It in effect robs us of quality of life.

There will be people or situations for which agreeing to try forgiveness will be far more difficult than others. We should expect that. But the measure of difficulty should not negate our willingness to keep on trying to forgive so we can move on. It's when we shut down and say we won't do it that we get ourselves into spiritual trouble. We have to remember that this thing called forgiveness is a spiritual ideal for which we will reach for our entire lives. *Are There Any Exceptions to the Rule?*

Sometimes, the thing or person before us seems too much like a leviathan in our lives. For some, it might be the rapist or murderer of a loved one. For others, it might be the unfaithful husband or wife. For still others, it might be an institution, like a hospital or even a government. Presumably, Timothy McVeigh and Terry Nichols found it impossible to forgive the American government for things done in its history, and their anger fueled them to a point of bombing the Murrah Federal Building in Oklahoma City. As an African American, I sometimes feel anger against the American government for things done to my people, and I imagine some Jewish people feel anger against the German government for the Holocaust. Lewis Smedes says we can't forgive institutions; the only things or people we can forgive are those who did something to us personally. That leaves me and perhaps others with the dilemma of how to handle the anger we may feel against the institutions, yet, we are mandated to never abandon the search of how to effectively handle the anger. Refusing to not forgive persons, circumstances, or institutions puts us out of the will of God. If we claim to love God, as most of us do, we have to be concerned about that.

As I write this, I am thinking about all the people who might be angry at even the suggestion that they forgive, given their situations. Then, I think about Jesus forgiving Peter, Judas, and Thomas. I think about the parents of Amy Biehl forgiving the youths who murdered their daughter. I think about Martin Luther King, who preached and practiced forgiveness of individuals and a government. I think of the woman who forgave the drunk driver who killed her only son. I think of Reginald Denny who forgave those who beat him almost to death. I think of the countless numbers of African Americans and Jews who forgave their tormentors though they never forgot (and should not forget) what was done to their ancestors.

Forgive Who?   Then, I think of the people who haven't forgiven anything or anyone.

The two groups are on opposite sides of a spectrum. On one side, there's a freedom to live and the ability to move on. On the other side, there's a heaviness that has kept too many people captive and miserable.

I've decided that though forgiveness is difficult and distasteful, I'd rather be on the freedom side of the spectrum. Life is just too short to have things otherwise.

Questions for Study

1. In your mind, are there exceptions to having to forgive? What are they? In the Bible story of Amnon, Tamar, and Absalom, what do you feel toward Absalom for taking Amnon's life?

2. Do you agree or disagree with Lewis Smedes that a person cannot forgive an institution? Why or why not?

3. Does it help to know what forgiveness includes and doesn't include (see examples in this chapter) as you consider the predicament you may now be in?

4. Does forgiveness preclude justice from taking place? Why or why not?

5. Do you hear about the importance of forgiving enough from your church, temple or synagogue? Would you like to hear more about it?

Notes

Introduction

1. Garrett Keizer, "The Other Side of Rage," *The Christian Century*, July–August 2002, p. 23.

Chapter 2

1. Keizer, p. 23.
2. Keizer, p. 23.

Chapter 3

1. Keizer, p. 23.
2. *The American Heritage Dictionary of the English Language* (Boston: Houghton Mifflin Company, 1978).
3. *American Heritage Dictionary.*

Chapter 5

1. Michael Henderson, "The Power of Forgiveness," *For a Change Magazine*, Online version, February-March, 2000, page 7.
2. Henderson, p. 8.
3. Paul Brand and Philip Yancey, *The Gift of Pain* (Nashville: Zondervan, 1997).
4. *American Heritage Dictionary.*

Chapter 6

1. Simon Weisenthal, *The Sunflower* (New York: Schocken, 1976).
2. Philip Yancey, *What's So Amazing About Grace?* (Grand Rapids: Zondervan Publishing House, 1997), p. 101.
3. Yancey, *Grace* p. 102.
4. Yancey, *Grace* p. 102-103.
5. Yancey, *Grace* p. 102.
6. Yancey, *Grace* p. 105.

Chapter 7

1. Yancey, *Grace* p. 119.
2. Yancey, *Grace* p. 120.

Chapter 8

1. Henderson, pp. 1-2.

Chapter 9

1. Walt Disney (based on book by Linda Woolverton, Robert Falls and Henry Hwang), *Aida*.
2. Lewis B. Smedes, *Forgive and Forget: Healing the Hurts We Don't Deserve* (San Francisco: Harper and Row, 1984), p xii.
3. Lewis B. Smedes, *The Art of Forgiving* (Nashville: Moorings Press, 1996), pp. 55-56.
4. Smedes, *Art*, pp. 55-56.
5. Philip Yancey, *Soul Survivor,* (New York: Doubleday, 2001), page 142.

Bibliography

The American Heritage Dictionary of the English Language. Boston: Houghton Mifflin Company, 1978.

Brand, Paul and Yancey, Philip. *The Gift of Pain.* Nashville: Zondervan, 1997.

Disney, Walt (based on book by Linda Woolverton, Robert Falls and Henry Hwang). *Aida.*

Keizer, Garrett. "The Other Side of Rage," *The Christian Century,* July–August 2002.

Smedes, Lewis B. *The Art of Forgiving.* Nashville: Moorings Press, 1996.

Smedes, Lewis B. *Forgive and Forget: Healing the Hurts We Don't Deserve.* San Francisco: Harper and Row, 1984.

Weisenthal, Simon. *The Sunflower.* New York: Schocken, 1976.

Yancey, Philip. *Soul Survivor.* New York: Dobleday, 2001.

Yancey, Philip. *What's So Amazing About Grace?* Grand Rapids: Zondervan Publishing House, 1997.